THE WISDOM LIBRARY OF MIKE MURDOCK

VOLUME 2

———✦———

THE ASSIGNMENT:

THE TRIALS & THE TRIUMPHS

AND

THE ASSIGNMENT:

THE PAIN & THE PASSION

TABLE OF CONTENTS

——————⟫•◦•⟪——————

THE ASSIGNMENT: THE TRIALS & THE TRIUMPHS

THE ASSIGNMENT: THE PAIN & THE PASSION

Unless otherwise indicated, all Scripture quotations are taken from the King James Version of the Bible.

The Wisdom Library Of Mike Murdock, Volume 2
Copyright © 2002 by **MIKE MURDOCK**
ISBN 1-56394-269-0/B-175
All publishing rights belong exclusively to Wisdom International
Published by The Wisdom Center · P. O. Box 99 · Denton, Texas 76202
1-888-WISDOM-1 (1-888-947-3661) · Website: **www.thewisdomcenter.tv**

THE WISDOM LIBRARY OF MIKE MURDOCK

VOLUME 2

THE ASSIGNMENT:
THE TRIALS &
THE TRIUMPHS

Everything Great Begins Small.

-MIKE MURDOCK

~ 1 ~

EVERY ASSIGNMENT HAS A BIRTHPLACE.

———————◆———————

Every Assignment Begins Somewhere.

Over the years, I have listened to extraordinary men of God speak. They can trace turning points of their life to a specific hour, a date, and a particular geographical place they were standing or kneeling.

This has happened in my own life. I can take you to the very spot where I first felt the call to preach the gospel. I was just four years old. It was in my father's church in Orange, Texas. A precious and godly woman, Lillian Logan, prayed for me. That morning in children's church, it was like fire inside me. I wept as I laid my little hands on the backs of the other children and prayed for them.

It happened again in Waco, Texas. I was just eight years old. I remember the moment. Even though the church has since been torn down, I remember where I was kneeling. Tears streamed down my face. I promised God, "I will go where you want me to go and be anything you want me to be."

Another life changing event occurred when I was fifteen years old. A great pastor, Fred Hill, was preaching at a camp meeting in Lake Arthur, Louisiana. In one of his sermons, he told a story about a little boy who came by the church every morning to pray for his parents who were not Christians. One morning after prayer, the pastor heard a crash and ran out to discover an automobile wreck outside the church door. The little boy had been killed.

At the funeral, both parents were saved. The pastor made this statement, *"The little boy did not live a long life, but he did live a full one."*

It tore me apart inside. I wept and sobbed the entire day. I had always felt like my time on earth was limited, and that I would not live out a full 70 or 100-year life span. That day I made a total commitment to God that however long my life might be, it would definitely be a *full* life—it would be dedicated to His glory.

Another turning point occurred when I was 18 years old in Bible school. A great missionary, R. L. Brandt, preached on the subject, "Burn your plow." He related that Elisha was *following* Elijah. Elisha had to stop his farming, *burn his plow* (his dependency upon his oxen for his financial income) and focus on his mentor's mantle.

As I listened that morning in chapel, conviction gripped me. You see, I had often felt that my financial income would derive from *business.* I would preach on *weekends.*

That day I surrendered to full-time ministry.

I spent the entire day weeping, laying on my face in that chapel. I felt that my heart was being torn out of my chest. I knew that total surrender meant that I could no longer depend on a business for my financial support. I had to be willing to empty myself completely to reach others with the gospel. Then, my trust in God would be validated and *rewarded.*

That was one of the most difficult days in my entire life. That was a time of very traumatic change in my life—I will always remember exactly *where* it took place.

The greatest day of my life was July 13, 1994.

I went to bed at 5:00 a.m. on Wednesday morning, July 13, 1994. I thought I would sleep in until 10:00 or 11:00 in the morning. But, after only two hours, at 7:00 a.m., I was awakened by the Holy Spirit.

I fell in love with Him that day.

The Holy Spirit forever changed my life and ministry. The Holy Spirit was so powerful and strong in my room that I was compelled to go to prayer. That day birthed an obsession—to intimately *know* the Person of the Holy Spirit—not just His power.

Since that day, I have held Schools of the Holy Spirit throughout the nation. I have found the Holy Spirit to be the only true Source of constant joy, and the only true Source of unchanging peace.

When I please Him, joy dominates me.

When I offend Him, He withdraws.

God will schedule uncommon experiences for you—you can have your own Bethel, Upper Room experiences and specific *places* that signal a total change in the direction of your life.

Document them.

Always celebrate turning points.

It is important for you to attach significance to the places where God speaks to you.

As I write these words to you, it is midnight on Wednesday. Here in the privacy of my little Wisdom Room in my home, the Holy Spirit has just nudged my heart to pray a special prayer for you, that your reading of this Volume on "The Assignment" will become the turning point of your life.

It is not a coincidence that this book is in your hand this very moment.

Your Assignment has a birthplace. Reading this book will be the beginning of a clear and understandable photograph of your Assignment on earth.

Our Prayer Together...

"Precious Holy Spirit, though it is late tonight as I am writing these words to my precious friend, You have stirred my heart to pray a special prayer. I ask You, in the holy name of Jesus of Nazareth, to touch my friend dramatically while he reads these words. Reveal clearly once and forever *the path to his Assignment.* Unmuddy his waters. Unclutter his life. Strip away from him every option and alternative to Your perfect plan. *Remove the distraction* from his life that breaks his focus. I decree from the north, the south, the east and the west, wonderful and rewarding people will step out of the shadows of his life and raise his arms during his personal battle for significance. Just as Aaron and Hur held up the hands of Moses during battle, place supportive relationships around him in the name of Jesus. Do this now. Holy Spirit, I ask You to walk beside my friend today. Carefully and methodically move him toward the *center* of his life Assignment. Unleash a new flow of energy and enthusiasm within him, so that he will embrace his Assignment with great joy and with new vigor and vitality. It is done this very hour. This is the birth place for his Assignment once and forever, in Jesus' name. Amen."

Remember: *Every Assignment Has A Birthplace.*

What You Make Happen
For Others...
God Will Make Happen
For You.

-MIKE MURDOCK

❧ 2 ❧

YOUR ASSIGNMENT WILL ALWAYS ENABLE SOMEONE ELSE TO SUCCEED.

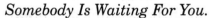

Somebody Is Waiting For You.

These Scriptures have greatly affected my life:

▶ "Knowing that whatsoever good thing any man doeth, the same shall he receive of the Lord, whether he be bond or free" (Ephesians 6:8).

▶ "Withhold not good from them to whom it is due, when it is in the power of thine hand to do it" (Proverbs 3:27).

▶ "The Spirit of the Lord God is upon me; because the Lord hath anointed me to preach good tidings unto the meek; He hath sent me to bind up the broken-hearted, to proclaim liberty to the captives, and the opening of the prison to them that are bound" (Isaiah 61:1).

Someone Should Succeed Because Of You.

Note that His empowering is to help other people around you *enter their Season of Greatness.*

The Assignment of *Ruth* was to Naomi. She was involved in Naomi's survival.

The Assignment of *David* was to help Saul and the Israelites enter victory. When he killed Goliath, he helped keep the nation of Israel free from domination by its enemies.

The Assignment of *Joseph* was the survival of the nation and his family. When Joseph interpreted Pharaoh's dream accurately, it enabled him to help his own family and thousands of people to survive through seven years of famine.

When *Job* prayed for his friends, God turned his own captivity and restored him.

Your Assignment has little to do with your personal survival.

It has much to do with helping others achieve total obedience to God's instructions. *When you help them, God gets involved with your life.*

As I was speaking on a telethon recently, the Holy Spirit spoke to me to tell the people something very powerful: "When you get involved with God's dream, He will get involved with *your* dream. When you get involved with what is on God's mind, He will get involved with what is on *your* mind. When the widow of Zarephath concentrated on the needs of the prophet—God concentrated on *her* needs."

It is quite true, *"What You Make Happen For Others, God Will Make Happen For You"* (read Ephesians 6:8).

When I talk to people about their Assignment, I always ask them this question: "Who is surviving today because of what you did last year?"

Remember: *Your Assignment Will Always Enable Someone Else To Succeed.*

≈ 3 ≈

YOUR ASSIGNMENT MAY BE REVEALED BY GOD THROUGH A DREAM.

God Often Speaks Through Dreams.

There are many strange occurrences in our lives that are unexplainable. Some dreams occur because you ate too much pizza at 2:00 a.m.! Other dreams occur because of a mixture of imaginations and fantasies we have entertained. However, some dreams come directly from God.

God has spoken to me through dreams on numerous occasions.

6 Important Facts You Should Remember About Dreams

1. *God Gave Joseph Dreams Of His Leadership And Promotion Years Before He Became Second In Command Of Egypt.* "And Joseph dreamed a dream, and he told it his brethren:" (Genesis 37:5).

2. *The Life Of Jesus Was Preserved By The Impartation Of A Dream.* Joseph, the earthly father of Jesus, received divine instructions through a dream. "And when they were departed, behold, the angel of the Lord appeareth to Joseph in a dream, saying, Arise, and take the young child and his mother, and flee into Egypt, and be thou there until I bring thee word: for Herod will seek the young child to destroy Him" (Matthew 2:13).

3. *Solomon Experienced Radical Changes Through The Flow Of Wisdom That Began Through A Dream.* "In Gibeon the Lord appeared to Solomon in a dream by night: and God said, Ask what I shall give thee." And Solomon answered Him, saying, "Give

therefore Thy servant an understanding heart to judge Thy people, And God said unto him, lo, I have given thee a wise and an understanding heart; so that there was none like thee before thee, neither after thee shall any arise like unto thee" (1 Kings 3:5,9,11,12).

4. *It Is Wise To Document Your Dreams.* Especially give attention to those which reoccur. Do not build your entire life-style around a dream, but rather let the dream be a motivation to pursue the presence of God and secure a clear-cut interpretation of what He revealed through that dream.

5. *Time Will Reveal The Validity Of Any God-Given Dream.* Several years ago, a young lady listened raptly as I spoke at a church here in Dallas. Afterwards, she came up to me and said, "I am assigned to you. Someday I am going to work for you and be your secretary."

"That is nice. I am certain God will guide your steps," I replied quietly.

To my surprise I arrived home a few weeks later and found she had become the secretary for my office manager. One day she whispered excitedly to me, "I still know I am assigned to you. I will be your personal secretary someday."

A few weeks later, through an unexpected turn of events, that position opened, and she was the one most qualified to fill it. She was excited. I thought, "Well, this is something! She said months ago that she was assigned to me. We shall see."

After thirty days of intense work and effort, she suddenly resigned. She could not handle the stress and strong demands of the position. I did not see her again for several years. Was she really assigned to me? Of course not.

6. *Evaluate Prayerfully And Patiently Any Dream You Believe To Be Divinely Inspired.* God gives us dreams to prepare us for a new season to increase our flexibility for making changes and move us closer to the center of our Assignment.

Remember: *Your Assignment May Be Revealed By God Through A Dream.*

☞ 4 ☜

YOUR OBSESSION WITH YOUR ASSIGNMENT DETERMINES THE SUCCESS OF YOUR ASSIGNMENT.

Success Requires Your Decision.
Failure merely requires your permission.

3 Necessary Elements In The Completion Of Your Assignment

▶ *Awareness* of your Assignment.
▶ *Development* of your Assignment.
▶ *Obsession* with your Assignment.

Your awareness of your Assignment may come through your parents. Samuel was a remarkable young man raised in the temple under the priest, Eli. He was one of the greatest men in the Old Testament. He anointed Saul. He anointed David to follow the kingship of Saul.

Hannah, the mother of Samuel, was one of the most remarkable women of the Old Testament. She wept and sobbed in the temple. "And she was in bitterness of soul, and prayed unto the Lord, and wept sore" (1 Samuel 1:10). This woman craved a child. She craved a man child, a *son*.

She was willing to take a vow to make it happen. It was a vow of isolation, loss and separation from the son. "And she vowed a vow, and said, O Lord of hosts, if Thou wilt indeed look on the affliction of Thine handmaid, and remember me, and not forget Thine handmaid, but wilt give unto Thine handmaid a man child, then I will give him unto the Lord all the days of his life, and there shall no razor come upon his head" (1 Samuel 1:11).

Wise parents continuously mentor their children regarding

their Assignment. Hannah brought Samuel to Eli. "And when she had weaned him, she took him up with her, with three bullocks, and one ephah of flour, and a bottle of wine, and brought him unto the house of the Lord in Shiloh: and the child was young. And they slew a bullock, and brought the child to Eli. And she said, Oh my lord, as thy soul liveth, my lord, I am the woman that stood by thee here, praying unto the Lord. For this child I prayed; and the Lord hath given me my petition which I asked of Him: Therefore also I have lent him to the Lord; as long as he liveth he shall be lent to the Lord. And he worshipped the Lord there" (1 Samuel 1:24-28).

▶ She explained her isolation from her son.

▶ She made Samuel aware of her vow and that he belonged now to God.

He was *required* to develop a life focused on the presence of God.

6 Action Steps In Developing An Obsession For Your Assignment

1. *Develop And Prepare For Your Assignment.* You are not *born* qualified—you must *become* qualified. Jesus took 30 years. Moses took 80 years. Preparation requires mentors, diligence and focus. "And Jesus increased in wisdom and stature, and in favour with God and man" (Luke 2:52).

2. *Develop An Obsession For Your Assignment.* The Apostle Paul is a perfect example. "Brethren, I count not myself to have apprehended: but this one thing I do, forgetting those things which are behind, and reaching forth unto those things which are before, I press toward the mark for the prize of the high calling of God in Christ Jesus" (Philippians 3:13,14).

3. *Become Ruthless In Removing Any Distractions To Your Assignment.* "So likewise, whosoever he be of you that forsaketh not all that he hath, he cannot be My disciple" (Luke 14:33). "For where your treasure is, there will your heart be also" (Luke 12:34).

4. *Never Consider Any Option To Your Assignment.* "And Jesus said unto him, No man, having put his hand to the plough, and looking back, is fit for the kingdom of God" (Luke 9:62).

5. *Expect God To Send Someone To You Who Makes You*

Aware Of Your Assignment. Abigail stirred the mind of David by reminding him of his destined place on the throne. He changed his plan from killing Nabal and his servants to awaiting God's timing (read 1 Samuel 25).

6. *Anticipate God Moving Quickly To Complete His Assignment Through You.* "Then said the Lord unto me, Thou hast well seen: for I will hasten My word to perform it" (Jeremiah 1:12).

One of the greatest healing evangelists in the world has often said, "God spoke to me and instructed me to bring his healing power to my generation." His *awareness* of his Assignment and his *obsession* to pray for the sick has created incredible success in his ministry.

If you succeed, it will happen because of your personal decision to obey God's voice.

If you fail, it will be through deliberate disobedience or ignorance of His plan for your life.

Nobody else is responsible for you. You are responsible for your own Assignment. Move quickly toward it.

Your *daily appointments* should reveal your obsession with your Assignment.

Your *friendships* should reflect your obsession with your Assignment.

Your *conversations* should revolve around your Assignment.

Remember: *Your Obsession With Your Assignment Determines The Success Of Your Assignment.*

Change Is Always
Proportionate
To Knowledge.

-MIKE MURDOCK

↝ 5 ↝

YOUR ASSIGNMENT MAY REQUIRE UNCOMMON KNOWLEDGE IN A SPECIFIC FIELD OF STUDY.

You Are Not Born Qualified.
You *become* qualified for your Assignment.

If God has called you to go overseas, study the culture, customs and language of that particular country.

If God has assigned you to the academic world, there may be areas of unique study that you have not even dreamed about pursuing. You must prepare yourself.

Qualification requires dedication. Prepare to focus hours of study and hard work. Be prepared to give up everything to complete God's Assignment in your life.

Do you really want to succeed in your Assignment? What are the necessary areas of study you must pursue?

It is quite interesting. Everywhere I go, people approach me and say, "I am called into the ministry. I cannot wait until God frees me from my secular job to go pursue His calling."

"Wonderful! I have an annual three-day School of Ministry at the Wisdom Center, and I would love to help train you for the ministry. It contains many hours of practical application in what you can presently do to move into your next season. Are you interested in coming?" I ask.

"Uh, uh, I will think about it. Right now, I am very involved in my business and building an extra room on my house. I am not sure I have enough money to fly to Dallas."

They are not taking their Assignment seriously. Or, they are totally mistaken about it.

I would not want anyone to work on my car who is unqualified.

I do not want anyone repairing my computers who is unqualified.

I do not want anyone teaching me the Word of God who is unqualified.

If you are unwilling to pursue knowledge of your Assignment, do not expect to succeed.

Remember: *Your Assignment May Require Uncommon Knowledge In A Specific Field Of Study.*

⇒ 6 ⇐

BECAUSE NOBODY ELSE HAS RECEIVED YOUR ASSIGNMENT, NOBODY ELSE UNDERSTANDS IT LIKE YOU DO.

Nobody Like You Has Ever Existed Before.

Nobody knows your Assignment like you do. This is why it is so important to find the center of your anointing and stay there. *Learn* your Assignment. *Focus* on it. Narrow down your life to build around it. Unclutter your life and get rid of anything that does not contribute to your Assignment. Do not dabble in everything. Specialize in what God has told you to do with your life. *Do it better than anyone else.* Do what you do best.

When I was fifteen years old, an extraordinary preacher came to visit our church. He was a magnificent and articulate speaker. I asked him to share with me important thoughts about the ministry. I will never forget it.

"First, anyone who reads less than 20 chapters a day of the Bible is not qualified to call himself a man of God," he said quite boldly.

So, at age 15, I began carefully studying 20 chapters of the Bible every day. I emptied myself into the Word of God, outlining five sermons per day from what I had read.

"How do you get such confidence when you get up to preach?" I asked.

"If I am going to speak on prayer," he answered, "I soak myself in prayer. I study the concordance and read every single Scripture I can find on the subject. I memorize Scriptures on prayer. I eat, drink and talk prayer 24 hours a day. I read every book written by great men of prayer. I find out their habits, their life-style and their comments. By the time I walk into the pulpit, I know more about prayer than any person sitting in front of me.

"Now, the audience does not even know what I am going to speak on that night. They have been on their jobs working as electricians, or engineers, or taxicab drivers. I have been studying *prayer.* I am many hours and many weeks *ahead of them.*

"I know that if any of them knew more about prayer than I do, God would have them in the pulpit instead of me. *So, when I get up to speak I am very aware that I know more about my subject than anyone else present.* That gives me boldness and confidence in my speaking."

This also explains why some of us do not succeed in our life. We are working on jobs that are not the *center* of our expertise. Perhaps we simply love our boss. Perhaps we just need work. We require finances to pay the bills, so we accept the first job available near our home.

This is tragic. Your Assignment should be unique to you. You cannot please anybody but the Lord. People will pull on you, trying to get you to follow their instructions. They will make demands on your time, your money and your attention. The only way to hear God's voice about your Assignment is to spend time alone with Him. Then empty yourself into what He told you to do with your life.

When God Places A Mantle On You, Nobody Else Can Do What You Do.

- ▶ Those Without Your Memories Cannot Feel Your Pain.
- ▶ Those Who Cannot Feel Your Pain May Not Understand Your Goals.
- ▶ Those Who Disagree With Your Goals May Disagree With Your Decisions.
- ▶ Those Who Are Angered By Your Decisions Are Potential Adversaries.
- ▶ Those Who Are Adversarial Toward You Are Unqualified To Receive Access To You.

Remember: *Because Nobody Else Has Received Your Assignment, Nobody Else Understands It Like You Do.*

∾ 7 ∾

YOUR ASSIGNMENT WILL BECOME YOUR LEGACY TO OTHERS.

———⇒⊃●⊂⇐———

You Will Be Remembered For Something.

When you hear the name Allan Greenspan, you think of the economy.

When you hear the name Adolph Hitler, you think of the holocaust.

▶ Your Assignment must become your *obsession*.

▶ Your Obsession will become your *legacy*.

▶ Your Legacy is the way you will be *remembered*.

Think for one moment. When you remember your mother, what one word describes her? When you think about your father, what one word describes him? When your children think about you, what one word will describe you?

Your life is not over.

You can make changes *today*.

Yes, even while you are reading this book, you can make significant changes in your life.

You can decide your legacy.

How do you want to be remembered by those closest to you? What is your plan for your future? What will be your legacy to those who follow after you? What provisions have you made for your influence to continue after you are gone? When people discuss you, what are the most common words they use? Who do you want to carry your mantle? Are you doing something worth perpetuating? Who are you training to take your place, carry your torch and create changes in the next generation?

You Will Be Remembered In Life For Two Things: The Problems You Solve Or The Ones You Create.

Jonas Salk will be remembered for the vaccine he discovered to cure polio. Mother Theresa is remembered for pouring her life out to the poor. Billy Graham will be remembered for the simplicity of the salvation messages he gave to millions. These great individuals solved problems.

This is their legacy—the way they are remembered.

12 Good Things About Problems

▶ *Your Assignment is to solve a problem.*
▶ The problem you solve is your legacy to others.
▶ Problems around you are the Golden Keys to favor.
▶ Problems can be marvelous, mysterious and wonderful Beginnings.
▶ Problems are the golden hinges on the Door of Relationship.
▶ Problems are Gateways to significance.
▶ Problems make people *reach* for each other.
▶ Problems create *humility,* forcing you to see the value of those around you.
▶ Problems begin new seasons.
▶ Your problem has birthed your financial income.
▶ *When you solve a problem, you create a reward.*
▶ *When you solve a problem for others, God guarantees your own prosperity* (see Isaiah 58:10,11).

You are commanded and expected to solve problems for others. "Withhold not good from them to whom it is due, when it is in the power of thine hand to do it" (Proverbs 3:27).

Focus only on the problems you are assigned to solve. Eliminate trivia from your day. Do not try to do too many things. Concentrate on pouring your life into a narrow focus, to solve the most significant problem possible for those closest to you.

Today can be the beginning of your greatness.

Remember: *Your Assignment Will Become Your Legacy To Others.*

≈ 8 ≈

YOU WILL ONLY BE REMEMBERED FOR YOUR OBSESSION.

The Persuaded Are Persuasive.

This is a strong statement. It is worthy of you sitting down this very moment while reading this book and contemplating, "What do I want to be *remembered* for?"

When you remember Alexander Graham Bell, you think about the telephone.

When you remember Thomas Edison, you think about the electric light bulb.

When you remember Henry Ford, you think about the automobile.

When you remember the Wright brothers, you think about the airplane.

When you remember Kathryn Kuhlman, you think about miracles.

When you remember George Washington, you think about the father of our country.

You will only succeed with something that has become an obsession.

Everything extraordinary began as a passion, a vision, an obsession.

Note anything that has the ability to keep your attention.

▶ Anything That Can Keep Your Attention Is Capable Of Mastering You.

▶ Focus Creates Mastery.

▶ What You Look At The Longest Will Become The Strongest In Your Life.

Some attempt careers in real estate. Yet, they hate to go to real estate seminars. They refuse to be mentored by someone who is already successful in that field. They refuse to invest inconvenient hours in showing properties to potential clients. Yet, they wonder why they do not succeed.

Late one night, I listened as two pastors of small churches discussed the reasons why their congregations remained small. It was interesting. One felt that it was because he "preached too straight."

When they finished talking I said quite simply, "Neither one of you has ever attended any church growth conferences. You buy houses and real estate and cars, yet you have never purchased an airline ticket to go and sit at the feet of a church authority who took a congregation to 4,000 people. Having 1,000 church members is not important to you because it has not become your obsession."

Your passion will become your legacy.

Remember: *You Will Only Be Remembered For Your Obsession.*

❧ 9 ❧

YOU WILL NEVER SEE THE MIRACLE HAND OF GOD IN ANYTHING YOU ATTEMPT WITHOUT HIM.

Your Assignment Will Require Miracles.

When God gives you an Assignment, it will require Him.

Never attempt anything great without God.

If God has not led you concerning your new business, do not start it.

If God has not led you into your relationship, stay single. Years ago, I was greatly pressured by friends to become engaged. Though I was not really "in love," I cared deeply for her. But, it was not right. In fact, I was not at all at peace that she was the person to marry. I permitted everyone else around me to talk me into the engagement.

The next morning my heart felt like ten thousand pounds of lead had been emptied on it. I had never known such a sudden lack of joy. I knew I had made a mistake. I had not received God's approval, but merely man's approval.

The approval of God is very necessary for anything you want to work in your life. Do not *force* relationships. *Let* them grow.

Provision is only guaranteed for the Assignment God has commanded.

Church leaders, please read this carefully. Satan is choking the life of the church through debt. One of the saddest pictures emerging is men of God who plunge their churches into debt, spending money that has never yet arrived. It seems a total contradiction to the instructions of the Word, "thou shalt not borrow" (Deuteronomy 28:12).

Whatever you are considering, if God is not in it, *refuse to do it.* Without the presence and blessing of the Lord, it will not bring you joy, but heartache.

Every command contains a plan. Find it.

Remember: *You Will Never See The Miracle Hand Of God In Anything You Attempt Without Him.*

≈ 10 ≈

EVERY STEP TOWARD SELF-SUFFICIENCY IS A STEP AWAY FROM GOD.

God Will Not Permit You To Succeed Without Him.

Many years ago I began to write songs. It was astounding how God blessed me. Suddenly people everywhere were recording my songs. I received tens of thousands of dollars in royalties.

Because I owned my own publishing company, I received double royalty as a composer and publisher. It was not long before I had built up quite a nest egg. I decided I would live off the interest the savings would generate.

One day in prayer, God spoke to me and said, *"Every step toward self-sufficiency is a step away from Me."* To this very day, I have never forgotten that word of warning.

God rewards faith, not brilliance. Moses wrote, "When thou hast eaten and art full, then thou shalt bless the Lord thy God for the good land which he hath given thee" (Deuteronomy 8:10). Then Moses went on to say, "And thou say in thine heart, My power and the might of mine hand hath gotten me this wealth. *But thou shalt remember the Lord thy God:* for it is He that giveth thee power to get wealth, that He may establish His covenant which He sware unto thy fathers, as it is this day" (Deuteronomy 8:17,18).

Our efforts are often attempts to create a life-style that will make God unnecessary. He will not permit that.

His Only Pleasure Is To Be Believed.

His Only Pain Is To Be Doubted.

Without faith, it truly is impossible to please the Lord.

You cannot succeed alone. "Not that we are sufficient of ourselves to think any thing as of ourselves; but our sufficiency is of God" (2 Corinthians 3:5). "Not of works, lest any man should boast" (Ephesians 2:9).

God has tested me numerous times. One Monday evening in a crusade, the Lord spoke to me and told me to give the entire offering to the pastor of the church where I was preaching. I did.

The Isaac Offering

Tuesday night, God instructed me to ask for eight people to plant a Seed of $1,000 in our ministry. After I made the announcement, eight people rushed to the front and stood there waiting. I anointed each of them with oil. We prayed, dedicating that Seed to the Lord. As we were praying, the Lord spoke to me and said, "This is an Isaac Offering."

The disappointment that hit my heart was indescribable. You see, an Isaac Offering is one when the Lord tells you to do something just to test your obedience. Then I instructed the people, "I know you are here to sow your Seed of $1,000. However, God has just spoken to me that this is an Isaac Offering. He just wanted to test your obedience to His voice. You are to keep your offering, and you will receive one hundredfold in return as if you had actually given it" (read Mark 10:28-30).

My $400,000 Seed

It happened again in one of my World Wisdom Conferences here in Dallas. An incredible wave of anointing swept into the service. I felt the Lord instructing me to have people come forward who would plant a Seed of $10,000 in our ministry to spread the gospel. Forty people rushed to the front to plant a $10,000 Seed. As I walked down the row and anointed each one, the Holy Spirit spoke to me and said very clearly, "I want this to be your Isaac Offering."

Now, as I just explained, an 'Isaac' Offering is when the Lord asks you to do something to test your *willingness*. Do you remember the story of Abraham and Isaac? After God had given Abraham his son Isaac through Sarah, He then asked Abraham to do a very hard thing: to sacrifice Isaac on the mountain.

Just as Abraham was about to kill Isaac, the voice of the Lord came forth. A ram was provided to replace Isaac. God just wanted to test his obedience to see whom he loved the most.

When I told the 40 partners of our ministry that it was an Isaac Offering, to keep the $10,000, and that God wanted just to test us, I went back with mixed emotions to my hotel room that night.

"That was $400,000 to buy television air time to spread Your name!" I argued. God spoke deeply into my spirit that night, saying, *"What You Are Willing To Walk Away From Determines What I Will Bring To You."*

Then, He spoke one of the most important Wisdom Keys that I have ever learned: *"Whatever You Can Walk Away From Is Something You Have Mastered."* Few people grasp this. But it has radically affected my life.

It is good to provide for your own household.

It is wise to plan ahead for your retirement.

It is honorable to carefully manage your money so that God is pleased. But do not ever forget: *Any attempt to isolate your life from acts of faith will be disastrous and will create catastrophes in your life.* Oral Roberts has said it well, "The most dangerous day in your life is the day you don't require a miracle."

God is only impressed by an act of faith.

Remember: *Every Step Toward Self-Sufficiency Is A Step Away From God.*

The Greatest Danger
Of Mercy
Is The Temptation
To Rebel Again.

-MIKE MURDOCK

❧ 11 ❧

GOD WILL NEVER ADVANCE YOU BEYOND YOUR LAST ACT OF DISOBEDIENCE.

Disobedience Will Paralyze Your Progress.

The great Israelite leader Joshua experienced this. "So the Lord was with Joshua; and his fame was noised throughout all the country" (Joshua 6:27). Everybody had heard about Joshua. Victories were being collected. The anointing and presence of God was manifest all over Israel.

Suddenly tragedy struck. "But the children of Israel committed a trespass in the accursed thing: and the anger of the Lord was kindled against the children of Israel" (Joshua 7:1).

Disobedience Turns God Into An Enemy.

Joshua had found the winning combination. His leaders were fierce fighters. His fame had been noised abroad. His mantle was secure. His leadership was extraordinary.

Suddenly, everything came apart.

The Israelites lost the battle of Ai. They were crushed. Their reputation unraveled. Joshua raced back to his tent and began to tear his clothes and cry out to the Lord. God then told him the reason they lost the battle. Disobedience was in the camp. One of his men, Achan, had kept some of the spoils from the city of Jericho, in direct disobedience to the Lord's commands.

God Can Become Your Enemy.

God can remove His Hedge of Protection.

Your tears will rush like Niagara Falls.

Your laughter stops.

Your victories become memories.

God can remind you of your frailty *in a single moment.*

This is seldom taught. We have such a "God loves you"

philosophy these days, that we have totally forgotten that the severity of the Lord is just as certain as His goodness. Hell is just as certain as Heaven.

When The Seeds Of Disobedience Are Planted, The Reward System Begins To Shut Down. Certainly, the mercies of God permit the blessings to fall like occasional rain drops. He attempts to keep you reminded of His mercy and His blessings. But continued disobedience eventually destroys your relationship with God.

That's why mercy often becomes dangerous.

When judgment is delayed, it is often misinterpreted. It is easy to assume that God did not really notice, that obedience is not that important, after all. Then, the judgment comes— swiftly and thoroughly.

My mother taught me an important truth.

"Son, the will of God is really an *attitude*." She continued, "If you get out of the will of God, if you will fall upon your face and cry loud to Him and ask Him to put you back in the center of His plan, in a single moment those blessings can begin to flow again."

Have you failed the Lord? Did you listen to the wrong person and sow a Seed of defiance and rebellion to God's plan? Please embrace this wonderful truth: A broken and contrite spirit He will not despise.

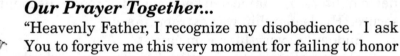 ### *Our Prayer Together...*

"Heavenly Father, I recognize my disobedience. I ask You to forgive me this very moment for failing to honor Your voice. I know I have sinned. This is not the direction I want my life to go. I give all of my life, my heart and my future to You today. Heal me on the inside. Heal my mind, my memories, my life. I embrace You as my Savior, my Lord and my God. From this moment forward, let Your mercy and peace flow toward me. Let today be the beginning of miraculous changes. From this day forward, I will walk uprightly toward You. In Jesus' name. Amen."

Stay obedient. Too much is at stake.

Remember: *God Will Never Advance You Beyond Your Last Act Of Disobedience.*

≈ 12 ≈

YOUR SUCCESS IN YOUR ASSIGNMENT DEPENDS ON YOUR ABILITY TO EMBRACE CORRECTION.

Only The Humble Are Correctable.

You do not know everything. Ignorance is devastating. "My people are destroyed for lack of knowledge:" (Hosea 4:6).

Your discoveries determine your seasons. The true difference between your present season and your future is information.

Correction hurts—when you try so very hard to do things correctly only to discover that you have made a bad decision. It especially hurts if those who are correcting you appear insensitive or unaware of your efforts.

16 Facts You Should Know About Correction

1. *Correction Was A Major Part Of The Ministry Of Jesus.*
    ▶ *Jesus corrected Peter.* "But He turned, and said unto Peter, Get thee behind Me, satan: thou art an offence unto Me: for thou savourest not the things that be of God, but those that be of men" (Matthew 16:23).
    ▶ *Jesus corrected the disciples.* "Afterward He appeared unto the eleven as they sat at meat, and upbraided them with their unbelief and hardness of heart, because they believed not them which had seen Him after He was risen" (Mark 16:14).
    ▶ *Jesus corrected Pharisees and Scribes.* "Woe unto you, scribes and Pharisees, hypocrites! for ye pay tithe of mint and anise and cummin, and have omitted the

weightier matters of the law, judgment, mercy, and faith: these ought ye to have done, and not to leave the other undone" (Matthew 23:23).

2. *Those Who Accepted The Correction Of Jesus Are Promised Everlasting Life.* "That if thou shalt confess with thy mouth the Lord Jesus, and shalt believe in thine heart that God hath raised Him from the dead, thou shalt be saved. For with the heart man believeth unto righteousness; and with the mouth confession is made unto salvation" (Romans 10:9,10).

3. *Those Who Rebelled Against The Correction Of Jesus Are Now Burning In Hell Forever.* "And in hell he lift up his eyes, being in torments, and seeth Abraham afar off, and Lazarus in his bosom" (Luke 16:23).

4. *The Apostle Paul Continuously Corrected Those Under His Spiritual Care.* The love of God within him motivated these letters of encouragement, correction and order. "All scripture is given by inspiration of God, and is profitable for doctrine, for reproof, for correction, for instruction in righteousness:" (2 Timothy 3:16).

5. *Prisons Are Filled With People Who Were Unwilling To Respect Correction.* Thousands will never see another rainbow during their lifetime, observe the gorgeous sunrise in the mornings, nor hear the laughter of children for the remainder of their life. Rebellion is always costly. "In the lips of him that hath understanding wisdom is found: but a rod is for the back of him that is void of understanding" (Proverbs 10:13).

6. *Corrections Should Begin Early In Life.* If you were fortunate enough to have parents who corrected you appropriately and continuously, your chances to succeed have been multiplied. "Train up a child in the way he should go: and when he is old, he will not depart from it" (Proverbs 22:6).

7. *Many Have Lost Valuable Years Of Mentorship Because They Are Unwilling To Take Correction From Their Pastor.* They move from church to church, looking for a "fresh" and new experience through a different man or woman of God. Stability has rewards beyond explanation. "Believe in the Lord your God, so shall ye be established; believe His prophets, so shall ye prosper" (2 Chronicles 20:20).

8. *Correction Is Your Bridge To Promotion.* "Give instruction

to a wise man, and he will be yet wiser: teach a just man, and he will increase in learning" (Proverbs 9:9).

9. *Reproof Can Position You Among The Successful.* "The ear that heareth the reproof of life abideth among the wise" (Proverbs 15:31).

10. *When You Refuse Correction, You Destroy Your Own Future And Life.* "He that refuseth instruction despiseth his own soul: but he that heareth reproof getteth understanding" (Proverbs 15:32).

11. *Counselors Increase The Potential Of Your Success.* "For by wise counsel thou shalt make thy war: and in multitude of counsellors there is safety" (Proverbs 24:6).

12. *Correction Can Eliminate Disappointments In Your Future.* "Without counsel purposes are disappointed: but in the multitude of counsellors they are established" (Proverbs 15:22).

13. *Godly Correction Increases Your Successes More Than The Love Of Another.* "Open rebuke is better than secret love" (Proverbs 27:5).

14. *You Can Predict The Success Of Your Children By Their Response To Your Correction.* "Correct thy son, and he shall give thee rest; yea, he shall give delight unto thy soul" (Proverbs 29:17).

15. *Correction Produces Wisdom In Your Child.* "The rod and reproof give wisdom: but a child left to himself bringeth his mother to shame" (Proverbs 29:15). "He that spareth his rod hateth his son: but he that loveth him chasteneth him betimes" (Proverbs 13:24).

16. *Correction Was Encouraged By The Ancient Wise Men.* "Hear instruction, and be wise, and refuse it not" (Proverbs 8:33).

It is sometimes difficult to differentiate between correction and criticism. It is often easy to accept correction from a proven mentor or a loyal friend. It is almost impossible to accept correction from a critic, an enemy or someone contemptuous of your Assignment. Accepting correction is the difference between maturity and immaturity.

Many years ago, a great military leader said, *"Observe thyself as your enemies would observe you, thus you will become your very best friend."* What did he mean? Look carefully at your life in the same way that the most critical, cynical and sarcastic enemy would examine you in an effort to destroy you. This enables you to discern the weaknesses in your life, your areas of vulnerability where your enemy could potentially destroy you.

Your best ideas may come from your worst enemy. Never forget this. As one of my dear friends, Sherman Owens, often says, "Listen to happy voices for *encouragement.* Listen to unhappy voices for *ideas.*" The unhappy customers are the ones who unlock the wisest changes made by great companies.

Your friends *accept* your weakness.

Your enemies *expose* your weakness.

Your mentor helps *remove* your weakness.

The Correction Checklist

Here is a short checklist to help you extract the most from those difficult, painful and sometimes tearful sessions of correction:

1. *Is It The Truth?* Truth sets you free. Truth makes change possible. Truth launches seasons of blessing. Correction is merely the painful hinge on the door to extraordinary pleasure. Correction is a moment; promotion can be a lifetime.

2. *If It Is Truthful, How Quickly Can I Make The Needed Change?* Who can encourage and strengthen me in making the change?

3. *If I Refuse To Accept This Correction, What Is The Worst Scenario That Could Eventually Occur In My Future?* How will it affect me financially? Socially? Emotionally? Spiritually? In my friendships and family? How will it affect those I love if I refuse to embrace the correction?

4. *What Prevents Me From Making This Change?* Am I willing to live with the limitations and consequences of my stubborn and rebellious decision?

5. *Am I Truly Thankful To God For The Correction?* Or, am I sullen, sulking and withdrawn?

6. *If It Is Not The Truth, Why Am I Upset?*

3 Tips On Receiving Correction From Those In Authority Over You

1. *Ask Them Routinely What Changes They Would Recommend That You Make To Complete Your Daily Tasks.*

2. *Make Them Your Mentors.* Invite them to schedule seminars, create book lists, etc. for you to improve your performance.

3. *Refuse To Focus On Their Lack Of Grace In Correcting You.* Instead, focus on maximizing and increasing your level of personal excellence.

3 Reminders When Giving Correction To Others

1. *Be Sensitive About The Timing Of Sharing Your Observations With Your Mate Or Members Of Your Family.* When people have difficult days at the office, patiently wait until the appropriate time to open your heart about making changes.

2. *Firmly, But Gently, Tell Them Your Feelings.* Be careful not to criticize them as individuals, but tell them how their behavior and conduct affected or offended you and why.

3. *Remind Them That You Too Welcome Their Observations And Explanations.* Success comes naturally to those who are willing to be mentored and corrected.

Some months ago, I saw a revelation in Scripture that intrigued me. I have always been a little shocked that Peter was so outspoken to Jesus. In fact, I have been shocked to see the uncouth, unchecked and ignorant response of Peter to the foot washing. "Peter said unto Him, Thou shalt never wash my feet" (John 13:8).

Then it dawned on me. Why would a loud-mouthed, brash and spontaneous fisherman feel so free to express his ignorant and sometimes stupid opinions in the face of Jesus? The answer is obvious. Jesus created a climate so free, relaxed and nonjudgmental that anyone could say anything he desired in His presence.

Jesus was not nervous around ignorant men.

Jesus was not intimidated by boisterous, brash and confrontational people.

Jesus permitted those around Him to say absolutely anything that came to their mind, good or bad, wise or stupid.

This enabled Him to quickly discern the level of their information, faith and maturity. Had He lived defensively, guardedly and in a constant posture of critical opinion, men would have been more guarded around him. Their true nature would have never surfaced, and effective ministry to them would have been impossible.

It is an interesting situation I observe around me now. There are people on my staff who are very easy to correct. They gladly make instant changes. They take giant steps toward their future.

Others, who are quite defensive, will even burst into tears at the slightest correction. I find myself withdrawing, withholding valuable suggestions from them fearing that they will become fragmented, demoralized and discouraged if I correct them.

So, I limit their responsibilities. I cannot make many changes in their agenda, nor recommendations to their daily life. They choose their own pace and mediocre routine, while maintaining a wonderful climate of love. Unfortunately, they will never taste the rewards of maximum greatness, nor experience the hundredfold fruits of prosperity. It is so unfortunate. I see it happen every day of my life.

Correction accelerates promotion, provision and leadership in your life.

Embrace it.

Cherish it.

And, thank God for the rest of your life that someone loves you enough to risk losing the friendship, in order to help you succeed.

Remember: *Your Success In Your Assignment Depends On Your Ability To Embrace Correction.*

⇌ 13 ⇌

YOUR ASSIGNMENT IS NOT TO EVERYBODY BUT TO SOMEBODY.

Everybody Does Not Need You.

But somebody does.

Moses was assigned to the Israelites. He was their Deliverer. "Come now therefore, and I will send thee unto Pharaoh, that thou mayest bring forth my people the children of Israel out of Egypt" (Exodus 3:10).

Aaron was assigned to Moses. He was his personal spokesman to the Israelites. "And the anger of the Lord was kindled against Moses, and He said, Is not Aaron the Levite thy brother? I know that he can speak well. And also, behold, he cometh forth to meet thee: and when he seeth thee, he will be glad in his heart. And thou shalt speak unto him, and put words in his mouth: and I will be with thy mouth, and with his mouth, and will teach you what ye shall do. And he shall be thy spokesman unto the people: and he shall be, even he shall be to thee instead of a mouth, and thou shalt be to him instead of God" (Exodus 4:14-16).

Ruth was assigned to Naomi. Naomi was her mother-in-law. "And Ruth said, Intreat me not to leave thee, or to return from following after thee: for whither thou goest, I will go; and where thou lodgest, I will lodge: thy people shall be my people, and thy God my God: Where thou diest, will I die, and there will I be buried: the Lord do so to me, and more also, if ought but death part thee and me" (Ruth 1:16,17).

Saul was assigned to rule over Israel. "Then Samuel took a vial of oil, and poured it upon his head, and kissed him, and said, Is it not because the Lord hath anointed thee to be captain over his inheritance?" (1 Samuel 10:1).

David was assigned to the Israelites. "And the Lord said unto Samuel, How long wilt thou mourn for Saul, seeing I have rejected him from reigning over Israel? fill thine horn with oil, and go, I will send thee to Jesse the Bethlehemite: for I have provided me a king among his sons" (1 Samuel 16:1).

Jonathan felt assigned to David. "Then Jonathan and David made a covenant, because he loved him as his own soul" (1 Samuel 18:3).

Your Assignment can be to merely one person, like Aaron to Moses.

Your Assignment may be to one *group* of people, like Moses to the Israelites.

But, your Assignment is never to everyone.

21 Keys That Reveal To Whom You Are Assigned

1. *When You Are Assigned To Someone, You Will Feel Their Pain When They Hurt.* Jesus is assigned to us as our Intercessor. "Seeing then that we have a great high priest, that is passed into the heavens, Jesus the Son of God, let us hold fast our profession. For we have not an high priest which cannot be touched with the feeling of our infirmities; but was in all points tempted like as we are, yet without sin" (Hebrews 4:14,15).

2. *When You Are Assigned To Someone, You Will Rejoice When They Rejoice.* "Rejoice with them that do rejoice, and weep with them that weep" (Romans 12:15).

3. *When You Are Assigned To Someone, Their Needs Matter More Than Your Own Needs.* "Then Esther bade them return Mordecai this answer, Go, gather together all the Jews that are present in Shushan, and fast ye for me, and neither eat nor drink three days, night or day: I also and my maidens will fast likewise; and so will I go in unto the king, which is not according to the law: and if I perish, I perish" (Esther 4:15,16).

4. *When You Are Assigned To Someone, God Will Anoint You With Supernatural Wisdom To Meet Their Needs.* "And Pharaoh said unto Joseph, I have dreamed a dream, and there is none that can interpret it: and I have heard say of thee, that thou canst understand a dream to interpret it. And Joseph said unto Pharaoh, The dream of Pharaoh is one: God hath shewed Pharaoh what He is about to do. And Pharaoh said unto Joseph, Forasmuch as God hath shewed thee all this, there is none so discreet and wise

as thou art: Thou shalt be over my house, and according unto thy word shall all my people be ruled: only in the throne will I be greater than thou" (Genesis 41:15,25,39,40).

5. *When You Are Assigned To Someone, You Will Possess Uncommon Patience Toward Them.* "We give thanks to God always for you all, making mention of you in our prayers; Remembering without ceasing your work of faith, and labour of love, and patience of hope in our Lord Jesus Christ, in the sight of God and our Father;" (1 Thessalonians 1:2,3).

6. *When You Are Assigned To Someone, You Will Leave Your Place Of Comfort To Minister To Them.* "And Ruth said, Intreat me not to leave thee, or to return from following after thee: for whither thou goest, I will go; and where thou lodgest, I will lodge: thy people shall be my people, and thy God my God: Where thou diest, will I die, and there will I be buried: the Lord do so to me, and more also, if ought but death part thee and me" (Ruth 1:16,17).

7. *When You Are Assigned To Someone, Their Enemies Become Your Enemies.* "And David spake to the men that stood by him, saying, What shall be done to the man that killeth this Philistine, and taketh away the reproach from Israel? for who is this uncircumcised Philistine, that he should defy the armies of the living God?" (1 Samuel 17:26).

8. *When You Are Assigned To Someone, Their Friends Become Your Friends.* "And Ruth said, Intreat me not to leave thee, or to return from following after thee: for whither thou goest, I will go; and where thou lodgest, I will lodge: thy people shall be my people, and thy God my God: Where thou diest, will I die, and there will I be buried: the Lord do so to me, and more also, if ought but death part thee and me" (Ruth 1:16,17).

9. *When You Are Assigned To Someone, Their Adversity Becomes Your Own Adversity.* "But Jonathan Saul's son delighted much in David: and Jonathan told David, saying, Saul my father seeketh to kill thee: now therefore, I pray thee, take heed to thyself until the morning, and abide in a secret place, and hide thyself: And I will go out and stand beside my father in the field where thou art, and I will commune with my father of thee; and what I see, that I will tell thee" (1 Samuel 19:2,3).

10. *When You Are Assigned To Someone, Their Vision Becomes*

Your Vision. "Then I told them of the hand of my God which was good upon me; as also the king's words that he had spoken unto me. And they said, Let us rise up and build. So they strengthened their hands for this good work" (Nehemiah 2:18).

11. *When You Are Assigned To Someone, Their Focus Becomes Your Focus.* It happened to Elisha. "And he left the oxen, and ran after Elijah, and said, Let me, I pray thee, kiss my father and my mother, and then I will follow thee. And he said unto him, Go back again: for what have I done to thee? And he returned back from him, and took a yoke of oxen, and slew them, and boiled their flesh with the instruments of the oxen, and gave unto the people, and they did eat. Then he arose, and went after Elijah, and ministered unto him" (1 Kings 19:20,21).

12. *When You Are Assigned To Someone, You Are Happy Every Time You See Them.* "Is not Aaron the Levite thy brother? I know that he can speak well. And also, behold, he cometh forth to meet thee: and when he seeth thee, he will be glad in his heart" (Exodus 4:14; also see 1 Corinthians 16:17,18).

13. *When You Are Assigned To Someone, You Are Willing To Give Them That Which Is Valuable To You To Convey Your Loyalty In Covenant.* "And Jonathan stripped himself of the robe that was upon him, and gave it to David, and his garments, even to his sword, and to his bow, and to his girdle" (1 Samuel 18:4).

14. *When You Are Assigned To Someone, You Will Risk Alienation From Others You Love To Protect The One To Whom You Are Assigned.* "Then Saul's anger was kindled against Jonathan, and he said unto him, Thou son of the perverse rebellious woman, do not I know that thou hast chosen the son of Jesse to thine own confusion, and unto the confusion of thy mother's nakedness? For as long as the son of Jesse liveth upon the ground, thou shalt not be established, nor thy kingdom. Wherefore now send and fetch him unto me, for he shall surely die. And Jonathan answered Saul his father, and said unto him, Wherefore shall he be slain? what hath he done? And Saul cast a javelin at him to smite him: whereby Jonathan knew that it was determined of his father to slay David" (1 Samuel 20:30-33).

15. *When You Are Assigned To Someone, You Have A Desire To Protect Them.* Jonathan felt this way about David. "And Jonathan said, Far be it from thee: for if I knew certainly that

evil were determined by my father to come upon thee, then would not I tell it thee?" (1 Samuel 20:9).

16. *When You Are Assigned To Someone, You Will Plead Their Cause To Their Enemies.* "And Jonathan spake good of David unto Saul his father, and said unto him, Let not the king sin against his servant, against David; because he hath not sinned against thee, and because his works have been to thee-ward very good:" (1 Samuel 19:4).

17. *When You Are Assigned To Someone, You Delight In Their Prosperity.* "Beloved, I wish above all things that thou mayest prosper and be in health, even as thy soul prospereth" (3 John 2). "Let the Lord be magnified, which hath pleasure in the prosperity of His servant" (Psalm 35:27).

18. *When You Are Assigned To Someone, Their Spiritual Condition Matters.* "And Philip ran thither to him, and heard him read the prophet Esaias, and said, Understandest thou what thou readest? And he said, How can I, except some man should guide me? And he desired Philip that he would come up and sit with him" (Acts 8:30,31).

19. *When You Are Assigned To Someone, You Willingly Expose Hidden Pain.* "For we would not, brethren, have you ignorant of our trouble which came to us in Asia, that we were pressed out of measure, above strength, insomuch that we despaired even of life:" (2 Corinthians 1:8).

20. *When You Are Assigned To Someone, You Will Risk Personal Loss To Guarantee Their Gain.* "And Jonathan answered Saul his father, and said unto him, Wherefore shall he be slain? what hath he done? And Saul cast a javelin at him to smite him: whereby Jonathan knew that it was determined of his father to slay David" (1 Samuel 20:32,33).

21. *When You Are Assigned To Someone, You Will Feel Uncommon Mercy And Forgiveness Toward Them.* "And he arose, and came to his father. But when he was yet a great way off, his father saw him, and had compassion, and ran, and fell on his neck, and kissed him" (Luke 15:20).

It is possible to attempt to help too many people. This explains why Paul declared, "but this *one* thing I do," (Philippians 3:13).

J. Paul Getty, the billionaire, once said, "I have seen as many people fail from attempting too many things as those who fail attempting too few."

How do you destroy a man with a great dream? Give him a second one. It will fragment his focus, dilute his energy and destroy his concentration.

You are not responsible *for* everyone.

You are responsible *to* someone.

Remember: *Your Assignment Is Not To Everybody, But To Somebody.* Find them.

☞ 14 ☜

YOUR ASSIGNMENT MAY BE TO ONLY ONE PERSON WHO WILL HAVE AN IMPACT ON MILLIONS OF OTHERS.

————————

No Assignment Is Small In The Eyes Of God.

Naaman was the captain of the armies of the king of Syria. Scriptures call him "a great man with his master, and honourable, because by him the Lord had given deliverance unto Syria: he was also a mighty man in valour, but he was a leper" (2 Kings 5:1).

Thousands of soldiers obeyed him. He had political clout. His advice and opinions were pursued. The husbands and sons of the entire country obeyed every instruction he gave. The king depended upon his counsel, courage and brilliant mind.

Unfortunately, he was a leper.

His wife had a maid. Nobody knows her name, even to this very day. The Scriptures did not even record it. She washed, folded and ironed clothes for a living. She was probably poor. Few sought her advice. Undoubtedly, she worked long hours each day.

But, she had compassion toward Naaman, her boss. She was quite aware of the man of God, Elisha, and the double portion anointing wrapped around his life. She was politically informed, perhaps because of overhearing conversations in the home of the captain. But, most important of all, she was spiritually informed and aware.

She was bold. She was confident. And, she spoke aloud her faith in the man of God. "And she said unto her mistress, Would God my lord were with the prophet that is in Samaria! for he would recover him of his leprosy" (2 Kings 5:3).

Somebody Close To You Can Often Connect You To Someone Who Can Change Your Life.

Naaman came with his horses and his chariot, and stood at the door of the house of Elisha. Elisha sent him a message to go and wash in Jordan river seven times and his leprosy would leave. Though angered by this instruction, Naaman eventually obeyed. "Then went he down, and dipped himself seven times in Jordan, according to the saying of the man of God: and his flesh came again like unto the flesh of a little child, and he was clean" (2 Kings 5:14).

The Assignment of one little housemaid affected others. "And he returned to the man of God, he and all his company, and came, and stood before him: and he said, Behold, now I know that there is no God in all the earth, but in Israel: now therefore, I pray thee, take a blessing of thy servant...for thy servant will henceforth offer neither burnt offering nor sacrifice unto other gods, but unto the Lord" (2 Kings 5:15,17).

▶ The captain of thousands declared a public covenant of commitment to God.

▶ His leaders, and even the ear of the king were now under the influence of a man touched by the hand of God.

▶ *The faith of one maid changed a nation.* "For who hath despised the day of small things?" (Zechariah 4:10). "Though thy beginning was small, yet thy latter end should greatly increase" (Job 8:7).

Even Jesus scheduled a visit to a city to have an appointment with just *one* woman. He sensed her need. This woman, who had been married five times, was like a magnet for his anointing. "And He must needs go through Samaria" (John 4:4).

It was there that He began a conversation at Jacob's well. Jesus initiated the conversation. "Give me to drink." None of the disciples were around because they had gone away into the city to buy meat. The woman was shocked. "Then saith the woman of Samaria unto Him, How is it that thou, being a Jew, askest drink of me, which am a woman of Samaria? for the Jews have no dealings with the Samaritans" (John 4:9).

Jesus explained that He would give her water. She would never thirst again. Then, He revealed that He knew she had had five husbands. The woman was spiritually awakened. "The woman then left her waterpot, and went her way into the city, and saith to the men, Come, see a man, which told me all things that ever I did: is not this the Christ?" (John 4:28,29).

One hurting woman was the Golden Connection to the people of the city. "Then they went out of the city, and came unto Him. So when the Samaritans were come unto Him, they besought Him that He would tarry with them: and He abode there two days. And many more believed because of His own word; And said unto the woman, Now we believe, not because of thy saying: for we have heard Him ourselves, and know that this is indeed the Christ, the Saviour of the world" (John 4:30,40-42).

Oh, my precious friend! Do not belittle any Assignment God has given to you at this time. You may feel that the crowds are applauding others. The glory of God is falling in other places where thousands have gathered. *But, your Assignment is as vital, vibrant and important as that of any other human on this earth.*

You must believe this *right now.* Embrace it.

Philip went down to the city of Samaria where Jesus had been talking to the woman at the well. Many were saved there. After the crucifixion, Philip was assigned to go there. The Bible says, "And the people with one accord gave heed unto those things which Philip spake, hearing and seeing the miracles which he did. For unclean spirits, crying with loud voice, came out of many that were possessed with them: and many taken with palsies, and that were lame, were healed" (Acts 8:6,7).

This is interesting. Jesus had visited the city.

Many believed Him.

Yet, many *remained* demon-possessed.

The Assignment of Jesus was the *woman.*

The Assignment of Philip was *the possessed.*

▶ *Your Assignment will always bring joy to someone.* "And there was great joy in that city" (Acts 8:8).

▶ *Your Assignment is always to a place.* In the midst of this tremendous wave of spiritual awakening, "And the angel of the Lord spake unto Philip, saying, Arise, and go toward the south unto the way that goeth down from Jerusalem unto Gaza, which is desert" (Acts 8:26).

▶ *Somebody needs you today and the Holy Spirit knows exactly where he or she is located.* "And he arose and went: and, behold, a man of Ethiopia, an eunuch of great authority under Candace queen of the Ethiopians, who had the charge of all her treasure, and had come to Jerusalem for to worship, Was returning, and sitting in his chariot read Esaias the prophet" (Acts 8:27,28).

▶*The Holy Spirit knows to whom you are assigned.* "Then the Spirit said unto Philip, Go near, and join thyself to this chariot" (Acts 8:29). He knows where they live.

He knows the questions you can answer in their lives.

You are a walking reward to those people.

Philip ran to him. He explained the gospel. Then he baptized the Ethiopian, "And when they were come up out of the water, the Spirit of the Lord caught away Philip, that the eunuch saw him no more: and he went on his way rejoicing" (Acts 8:39).

According to some historians, 90 percent of Ethiopia came to Christ through the testimony of this eunuch. The Holy Spirit spoke to *one man*, Philip, to go meet *another man* in the desert. Revival broke out, and *thousands* came to Christ.

Do not despise what appears to be a trivial Assignment. Nothing is small to God—absolutely nothing. If He made it, it is important to Him.

Whatever your present Assignment may be, cultivate *excellence* in it. Do it right. Do the best you can at this time. Abandon yourself to *completing* it.

Something bigger than you have ever imagined is on the other side of this Assignment.

Remember: *Your Assignment May Be To Only One Person Who Will Have An Impact On Millions Of Others.*

～ 15 ～

GRATITUDE IS OFTEN A CONFIRMATION OF YOUR ASSIGNMENT.

Any Drowning Man Appreciates A Life Jacket.
Many need you.
Few appreciate you.

Those few, to whom you have been assigned, will confirm it through their respect and appreciation of you.

This explains the instructions of Jesus to His disciples. "And into whatsoever city or town ye shall enter, inquire who in it is worthy; and there abide till ye go thence. And when ye come into an house, salute it. And if the house be worthy, let your peace come upon it: but if it be not worthy, let your peace return to you. And whosoever shall not receive you, nor hear your words, when ye depart out of that house or city, shake off the dust of your feet" (Matthew 10:11-14).

Many people needed miracles in the days of Jesus. Why did He stop for a blind man sitting by the highway begging? Jesus had a schedule. He had appointments. He had His disciples and a great number of people around Him.

The blind man discerned His value.

The responsiveness of the blind man attracted Jesus. "And many charged him that he should hold his peace: but he cried the more a great deal, Thou son of David, have mercy on me. And Jesus stood still, and commanded him to be called. And they call the blind man, saying unto him, Be of good comfort, rise; He calleth thee" (Mark 10:48,49).

The woman with the issue of blood appreciated Jesus. She had suffered for 12 years. The Bible said she had suffered "many things of many physicians." She had spent every cent she had.

She had never improved. In fact, the Bible says she "grew worse" (read Mark 5:25,26).

When she heard of Jesus, she pressed in behind Him and touched His garment. Listen to her incredible faith, her confidence in Jesus and her appreciation. "For she said, If I may touch but His clothes, I shall be whole. And straightway the fountain of her blood was dried up; and she felt in her body that she was healed of that plague" (Mark 5:28,29).

▶ Who is *responsive* to your presence?

▶ Who *celebrates* every word you speak?

▶ Who responds *swiftly* to your instruction?

▶ Who prefers your presence to all others?

▶ Who is reluctant to leave your side?

Clues are plentiful. Note them.

Remember: *Gratitude Is Often A Confirmation Of Your Assignment.*

∾ 16 ∾

THE ONE WHOSE SUCCESS MATTERS TO YOU THE MOST IS THE ONE TO WHOM YOU ARE ASSIGNED.

Somebody's Success Should Be Your Obsession.

Who is it? Whose success stays on your mind *all the time?* What person or group of people consume your thoughts?

This is a clue to whom you have been assigned.

God has you on His mind all the time. Listen to David. He is well aware of the love of God toward him. "How precious also are Thy thoughts unto me, O God! how great is the sum of them! If I should count them, they are more in number than the sand: when I awake, I am still with Thee" (Psalm 139:17,18). God sees you as His Assignment. You are on His mind every moment of the day!

God has even assigned angels to you. "But to which of the angels said He at any time, Sit on My right hand, until I make thine enemies thy footstool? Are they not all ministering spirits, sent forth to minister for them who shall be heirs of salvation?" (Hebrews 1:13,14).

Those whose success matters to you the most are those to whom you have been assigned.

A father watches silently as the young lady receives the crown at a national beauty pageant on television. He sips his tea. Then, he calmly walks to the kitchen to eat supper. But, when his daughter calls and says, "Daddy, I got a raise on my job!" He beams. He smiles. He tells all his friends at work that his daughter got a promotion. *She is his Assignment.*

Parents are assigned to their children.

Here is a powerful and important self-test: When a child

comes home from school shouting and thrilled over something wonderful occurring in their life, you should feel great joy. If you do not, it is a signal that your focus is not on your Assignment. This must be corrected. If you are more excited over the success of a neighbor than that of your own children, you have failed to acknowledge and discover the center of your own calling.

Thousands of children are being damaged because parents have not embraced their personal Assignment. What can you do? Talk to the Holy Spirit. Confess that something within you has been broken. Your heart needs mending again. Your mind needs renewing. It may be damaged through strife and difficult seasons. Perhaps, your own parents neglected you, and you do not know how to reach out and strengthen your family. Stay teachable. The healing can begin this very moment, even while you are reading this book.

It is possible that satan will use a bitter experience to break your focus and derail you. Only in the presence of the Holy Spirit can that be revealed to you. Only with a humble heart will you be able to make the appropriate changes and bring great joy again to your life.

The Apostle Paul received joy at the victories of others. "For ye are our glory and joy" (1 Thessalonians 2:20). So, note those whose triumphs and victories bring you joy.

Remember: *The One Whose Success Matters To You The Most Is The One To Whom You Are Assigned.*

❧ 17 ❧

GOD IS CONSTANTLY SCHEDULING GOLDEN CONNECTIONS TO ADVANCE YOUR ASSIGNMENT.

God Can Link You With Anyone Within 24 Hours.
Never forget this. God knows *exactly* where you live. He is fully aware of every human on this planet. Look at the life of Ruth. She went from the peasant fields of Boaz to being his wife in a single day.

Golden Connections are those people who become Divine Bridges that enable you to exit from one season and enter into the next Season of Blessing. The butler was a connection for Joseph to personally meet Pharaoh and interpret his dream.

No relationship is insignificant in your life.

God Is Committed To The Completion Of Your Assignment. "The Lord will perfect that which concerneth me:" (Psalm 138:8). "Being confident of this very thing, that He which hath begun a good work in you will perform it until the day of Jesus Christ:" (Philippians 1:6).

13 Wisdom Keys You Should Know About The Golden Connection Of Your Life

1. *You Cannot Succeed Without Golden Connections.* Your Creator planned it. He wanted you to know others. "And the eye cannot say unto the hand, I have no need of thee: nor again the head to the feet, I have no need of you" (1 Corinthians 12:21).

There is an interesting Scripture from the Apostle Paul. He

describes how each of us fit together. "From whom the whole body fitly joined together and compacted by that which every joint supplieth, according to the effectual working in the measure of every part, maketh increase of the body unto the edifying of itself in love" (Ephesians 4:16). Relationships increase us. Multiply us.

2. *When God Wants To Bless You, He Brings A Person Into Your Life.* Look for them. Expect them. Discern them. Be swift to respond to them. "Two are better than one; because they have a good reward for their labour" (Ecclesiastes 4:9).

3. *Your Golden Connection May Not Be Outwardly Appealing.* God uses burlap bags sometimes to carry His Gold Bars of Blessing. The camels of Abraham were not appealing, but they carried the wealth of the patriarch. When Rebecca agreed to water the camels, she connected with Isaac, her wealthy husband-to-be.

Ruth was a Moabite girl, a heathen. But she was Boaz's connection to the lineage of Jesus. Jephthah, a great leader, was thrust out by his family. Jephthah was the son of a harlot. But he was the Golden Connection that brought deliverance to the people of God.

4. *Do Not Reject A Golden Connection Because It Does Not Meet Your Qualifications For An Intimate Relationship.* Let me explain. The butler may not have been received by Joseph to be a best friend. But he was The Golden Connection to the throne. The Apostle Paul did not want to be shipwrecked on the island of Melita. But God used it as a Divine Connection with the leader of the island, Publius. His father was healed through Paul's ministry. These were Divine and Golden Connections that had been scheduled by God.

5. *Crisis Always Brings Good People Together.* Expect to find gold in every fiery furnace of your life. Best friends often come together through disasters and tragedies. Many times I have heard the remark, "This is my best friend. We met during a crisis."

Some time ago I read some statistics on relationships. According to the report, you are just four people away from any human on earth. This means that *you* know someone...who knows *another* person...who knows a third person...who is connected to *anyone you could possibly meet* on earth. This includes leaders of nations and CEOs of corporations. God can get anyone to you anywhere you are.

6. *Recognize That God Often Uses Illogical Methods And Unlikely People To Help Fulfill Your Assignment.* I have often said that if you can figure something out, God is probably not in it. God is a supernatural, miracle working God.

Picture the Ethiopian eunuch. He is puzzled and bewildered. He desperately needs a Divine Connection with the man of God. "Then the Spirit said unto Philip, Go near, and join thyself to this chariot. And Philip ran thither to him," (Acts 8:29,30). Yes, God can get The Golden Connection to you within 24 hours.

7. The *Golden Connection* Is Not Necessarily Your Best Friend. As you recall, the butler forgot Joseph for two years after his exit from the prison!

8. The *Golden Connection* May Not Necessarily Feel Loyal To You. The Connection may not even consider you essential or even desirable.

9. The *Golden Connection* For Your Life May Have Flaws Repulsive To You. Yet, God will use their difference or gift...to bless you.

10. The *Golden Connection* May Not Be A Mentor Nor A Protégé.

11. The *Golden Connection* May Depart From Your Life, Never To Be Seen Again After God Uses Them.

12. The *Golden Connection* May Be Used By The Holy Spirit To Move You From A Place Of Loss To A Place Of Favor.

13. *Someone Is Always Observing You Today Who Is Capable Of Greatly Blessing You Tomorrow.* Remember Ruth. Boaz was discussing her with his employees weeks before she even knew he noticed her. Somebody is discussing your promotion this very moment. Somewhere in the seat of power and decision-making, your name is being considered. Get your faith up! Sow Seeds of Expectation every day!

God is planning something so big that no devil can stop it— The Golden Connection.

Remember: *God Is Constantly Scheduling Golden Connections To Advance Your Assignment.*

Nothing Is Ever As It First Appears.

-MIKE MURDOCK

☞ 18 ☜

YOUR PRESENT ASSIGNMENT MAY MERELY BE A BRIDGE TO A GREATER SEASON.

Your Present Situation Is Probably Temporary.

Joseph stayed aware of this at all times. It preserved his mind. It kept him focused. He never accepted his present trial as a permanent place. That is why he told the butler returning to the palace, "But think on me when it shall be well with thee, and shew kindness, I pray thee, unto me, and make mention of me unto Pharaoh, *and bring me out of this house.*" (Genesis 40:14).

Naomi was an Assignment for Ruth. However, Naomi was The Golden Connection to Ruth's husband, Boaz (see Ruth 1-4).

Never despise where God has placed you. He has a master plan and blueprint for your life. It is a *wise* plan. It will *benefit* you. Your present season is merely a Bridge, a Connection, a Gate to something so wonderful He cannot even tell you all the details yet.

It is tempting to become agitated when the benefits of the present season seem exhausted. It was this sin that robbed the Israelites from their reward of Canaan.

They complained in Egypt.

Then, they complained in the wilderness.

They complained continuously.

Golden Connections are created ahead of time. You must believe that God has scheduled your present situation. It contains purpose and benefit. You must determine to stay there long enough for Him to complete His Assignment.

You must exhaust the benefits of your present before God will promote you into your next season.

You may never pass this way again.

Take a sheet of paper and draw up an inventory of your present season: the *benefits* of your present circumstances. Do not yet create a list of the disadvantages, pain and lack of benefits. Rather, make a detailed inventory of what God has *presently* provided for your life.

What complimentary or free benefits do you receive? Who are the people you have access to today who possess something you need, desire or respect? What knowledge is close to you that you have not yet pursued? What currents of favor are presently flowing toward your life from others?

Drop your bucket in the Well of the Present and draw out water continuously. As I told a young travel assistant once, "Son, I am paying your airline tickets to fly all across the world. I am paying for your hotel bills, your food bills, luggage and clothing. You are being introduced to the highest caliber of humans known on earth. You are permitted to sit in the counsel of brilliant people. Every single day of your life, you hear the teaching of a proven man of God. You eat the greatest food ever cooked on earth in the finest restaurants possible. You may never pass this way again. Stop complaining about long hours, and inventory the benefits of the present season that may never occur again the rest of your life."

Are you going through a difficult season? Have you developed bitterness? Anger? Cynicism? These must be burned out of your heart by the presence of the Holy Spirit. Move toward Him today.

Is your present season a battle? Extract every possible benefit from it.

Bad times bring good people together. It was in the *starvation* season that the widow of Zarephath connected with the greatest man of *faith* in her generation. It was during false accusation that Joseph met the butler, the confidant of Pharaoh who made him Prime Minister. It was while Ruth was gleaning in fields and gathering barley for a widowed mother-in-law, that she was observed by Boaz, the wealthy man of her city, who eventually married her.

Your Greatest Relationships Are Often Birthed In The Darkest Seasons Of Your Life. When Saul reacted badly toward David, the heart of Jonathan was knit with him. Their friendship was the golden example of what God intended for humans to experience.

So, when things are going worse than ever in your life, the most incredible relationships are near and ready to enter.

Your present season will pass. "Behold, I will do a new thing; now it shall spring forth; shall ye not know it? I will even make a way in the wilderness, and rivers in the desert" (Isaiah 43:19).

Your present season may seem like the fiery furnace of the three Hebrew children.

You will pass *through* this season.

You will pass through your present darkness.

You will move on to the next season of *increased provision and blessing.* "Fear not: for I have redeemed thee, I have called thee by thy name; thou art Mine. When thou passest through the waters, I will be with thee; and through the rivers, they shall not overflow thee: when thou walkest through the fire, thou shalt not be burned; neither shall the flame kindle upon thee" (Isaiah 43:1,2). "Whereas ye know not what shall be on the morrow. For what is your life? It is even a vapour, that appeareth for a little time, and then vanisheth away" (James 4:14).

Remember: *Your Present Assignment May Merely Be A Bridge To A Greater Season.*

Your Respect For Time
Is A Prediction Of
Your Financial Future.

-MIKE MURDOCK

❧ 19 ❧

EACH MOMENT IS AN OPPORTUNITY TO ADVANCE IN YOUR ASSIGNMENT.

One Moment Can Make A Difference.

Time is *so* precious. It is impossible to save, store or gather Time. You must simply learn the best ways to invest it.

Moments really do matter. The Apostle Paul treasured time. "See then that ye walk circumspectly, not as fools, but as wise, Redeeming the time, because the days are evil" (Ephesians 5:15, 16).

Time is the currency of earth. Mexico has the peso. France has the franc. Germany has the mark. The United States has the dollar. God has given a currency to us here on earth—the currency called Time.

Think about this. God did not simply give you friends. He gave you *Time.* You accepted Time and invested Time back into people. That produced friendships. God did not simply give you money. He gave you *Time.* You offered your Time to an employer and traded your Time for his money. You took the money and purchased your home.

Time is one of the most precious and valuable gifts God has given to you.

Study the success habits of uncommon achievers. You will notice one obvious and outstanding quality. All champions and leaders are very conscious of time. They wear watches. They continually consult them. When you have an appointment with them, they establish the perimeters of the appointment. Boundaries are set. You simply do not meet someone at 3:00 p.m. You will meet with them from 3:00 p.m. until 3:30 p.m.

Why is this? Their Time is the most precious commodity in

their life. It is the currency of time that helps them strengthen their families, birth ideas and achieve their dreams and goals.

I must make something very clear to you if I am to help you achieve your Assignment. There are people who are poor by the standards of today. Many of those who are struggling have a common thread—an obvious disrespect for time.

They are late for appointments.

They do not have a written plan for each day.

Conversations are vague instead of focused.

Your Respect For Time Is A Prediction Of Your Financial Future. I read an interesting illustration many years ago. If you have five pounds of iron, you can use it three different ways:

1)   It can be used to make *horseshoes.* If so, it would be worth approximately $10.

2)   You can use the five pounds of iron to make *needles.* In this form, it would be worth approximately $300.

3)   You can use the iron to make *watch springs.* In that form, it would be worth thousands of dollars. The same amount of iron, used three different ways, will produce three different levels of financial income.

Your time is much like this bar of iron. You can watch a television movie for two hours. Or, you can read and absorb the financial success secrets from the biography of a billionaire. You can sit at your table and eat a meal for ninety minutes and talk with your friends. Or, you can eat for 30 minutes and go walk four miles in the following 60 minutes. You decide.

▶ *Champions Make Decisions That Create The Future They Desire.*

▶ *Losers Make Decisions That Create The Present They Desire.*

You must cultivate a total focus on your Assignment. Remember, you will only succeed with something that is an obsession. Last night, I was readying the biography of the fascinating entrepreneur of our generation, the late Sam Walton, head of the Wal-Mart stores. Throughout the book, he continuously referred to the fact that he was obsessed with retailing.

He spent *every available moment* studying retail sales.

Those moments paid off.

7 Keys In Making Moments Count

1. *Keep A Calendar Or Day Planner With You At All Times.* What You See Determines What You Desire. Someone has well said, "A short pencil is better than a long memory." God instructed us, "Write the vision, and make it plain upon tables, that he may run that readeth it" (Habakkuk 2:2).

Your day planner should be handy and kept with you always. If it is too large, you will use its size as an excuse to leave it at home, or in the car. At first, carrying *anything* will become uncomfortable. However, remember that it is your blueprint for the dreams and goals of your life. Others may sit around and discuss the weather, the wind or current news.

You are on an Assignment.

You are focused.

2. *Stay Aware Of Each Hour As It Occurs.* Develop precision with each appointment. "For the vision is yet for an appointed time, but at the end it shall speak, and not lie: though it tarry, wait for it; because it will surely come, it will not tarry" (Habakkuk 2:3).

3. *Review The Appointments And Plans Of Each Day Continually.* Visualize them as links to your eventual goal and dream.

4. *Read Continuously.* When I am in an airplane, waiting at the airport or sitting in a taxi, I *read.* I read newspapers, magazines, books or my Bible. I try to absorb everything related to my Assignment. Occasionally, I will read a novel for relaxation. When I do, I have a pen in hand to circle anything in that novel linked to something I want to do with my life.

Extract an education from events, people and reading material around you. *Cultivate* that kind of appetite, even if you are not born with it.

Clip articles out of newspapers. Tear pages out of magazines, and build files—anything to strengthen your resolve and focus on the Assignment God is burning into your life.

5. *Listen. Listen. Listen.* While listening, ask questions. When you are with a lawyer, ask him which three most important things he feels you should know. When you are visiting a Realtor,

ask him the three most important characteristics of buying and selling a home. When you are with your pastor, ask him the three most important daily habits necessary for birthing a powerful, relationship with God.

6. *Ask Questions That Control The Focus And Quality Of Every Conversation.* Keep a legal pad and a pen or a microcassette with you at all times. There is probably never a moment I do not have a microcassette in my hand or pocket, or a legal pad. Why? *One idea could birth a million miracles.*

I have a very special friend who is quite successful. Every word that comes forth from his lips is like gold. In his presence, I am rejuvenated and invigorated, and I become quite imaginative. When he talks, things happen within me. It is like fireworks going off. When I am in his presence, time does not matter. Why? He gives me something I cannot get anywhere else. So, I keep my recorder and paper busy every time we are together.

I cannot afford to waste a minute of my time doing something unrelated to my Assignment. You, too, must make every moment count in your life.

7. *Enter Into Conversations That Advance Your Assignment.* Keep focused. Occasionally, I have people approach me and want to talk about things unrelated to my calling. I simply refuse. Why? I am ruthless in protecting my focus on the Assignment God has placed in my life.

Someone called my office a few weeks back. "Hello, Mike! I want to discuss a business proposition with you!"

"Does it have anything to do with the Wisdom of God?" I asked.

"Not really, but I am loving it, and want to sit down for a day and share it with you."

"I am sorry, but my present Assignment from God is taking up 24 hours a day, seven days a week and 365 days a year. When I feel His Assignment changing in me, I will telephone you!" I graciously hung up.

If I returned every telephone call, answered every single question asked of me, flew to every city where someone had requested me, listened to every cassette mailed to me, or read every book handed to me, I would not have time to live one single day of my life properly.

Every moment is valuable. You have nothing to give to those who disrespect your time.

Access to God was His first gift to you.

Time was His *second* gift to you.

Do not squander it in any way. It is the precious gift of time that enables you to enter into The Secret Place, read the Word of God and do what He has assigned you to do.

When a young lady met me at a restaurant for our date, she was 45 minutes late. She laughed it off. I could hardly believe how lightly she considered time. Obviously, the relationship did not work out.

Your respect for time will always distance you from others.

Disconnect from people who do not appreciate your time. Several years ago, I flew 1,500 miles to a crusade. It was a Saturday evening. I was speaking Sunday, both morning and night. Then, I would fly back home Monday afternoon. It involved three days of my life in a strange motel room, away from my home and family. The pastor leaned over to me Sunday night and whispered, "Could you get us out within 40 minutes?"

"I can get you out right now," I replied. "If you have flown me here 3,000 miles for three days and do not desire more than 40 minutes of Wisdom, I am in the wrong place anyway." I have refused to return to that church.

When you see somebody who is flippant and careless with their time, know they will be flippant and careless with your time as well. I have seen people come and sit around my offices and ministry doing very little, then ask me for a job. If they are careless with their own hours, imagine what they would do working for me.

I replied to a resume once. Nobody answered the telephone. I was surprised that an answering machine did not accommodate me. When I finally talked to the job applicant, I asked, "Why do you not have a telephone answering machine?"

"I do not like answering machines," was her reply.

Obviously, I would not even consider hiring someone who was that insensitive to time. What did that tell me? Her friends' time did not matter. She forced everyone to keep returning phone calls to reach her. When someone telephoned her, they were unable to leave any messages. Consequently, they wasted their entire effort, time, energy and finances. I could not afford to have someone so thoughtless on my payroll.

I would be reluctant to hire anyone who wrote me long 15 page letters. Why? Their time does not matter. They refuse conciseness. They force their friends to read trivia and absorb nonessential information—simply because they do not want to think before writing.

I have sat for several hours in the presence of young preachers who are launching their ministries. Few have ever asked me one serious, thoughtful and important question. Oh, how we waste the time God has given to us! Time is a wonderful and glorious tool God has given you to build your dream, your goals, and your Assignment. Do not throw it away.

"To every thing there is a season, and a time to every purpose under the heaven: A time to be born, and a time to die; a time to plant, and a time to pluck up that which is planted; A time to kill, and a time to heal; a time to break down, and a time to build up; A time to weep, and a time to laugh; a time to mourn, and a time to dance; A time to cast away stones, and a time to gather stones together; a time to embrace, and a time to refrain from embracing; A time to get, and a time to lose; a time to keep, and a time to cast away; A time to rend, and a time to sew; a time to keep silence, and a time to speak; A time to love, and a time to hate; a time of war, and a time of peace" (Ecclesiastes 3:1-8).

Remember: *Each Moment Is An Opportunity To Advance In Your Assignment.*

RECOMMENDED BOOKS AND TAPES
B-127 Seeds Of Wisdom On Goal-Setting (32 pages/$5)

❧ 20 ❧

YOUR ASSIGNMENT IS ACTUALLY AN HOURLY EVENT.

Maximize Today.

Yesterday is already over, so it really does not exist anymore. It is in the past. It is over. It is in the tomb. Tomorrow is in the womb. It has not been born yet. It is not here. It really is not your life because you have not seen it yet.

Your life is today.

This may sound a little strange, but you really will never *see* the future. Ever. When you arrive in your future, you will rename it "today."

Three years ago, you may have made a declaration, "In three years, I will be doing such and such." Well, you are here. This is three years later. Yet, what are you doing *today*? Are you still talking about your *future*? Are you still talking about what you will do five years from now? You will never get there. Never.

When you get into your future, you will rename it "today."

The Key to Life is discerning the essentials of The Perfect Day, and making it happen habitually.

The Perfect Day

Several years ago, the Lord gave me an interesting picture while I was on a fast. I saw my life as a Golden Train on the Track of Success. In my "future", I saw Cities of Achievement along the track. My Golden Train of Life was racing toward those Cities of Achievement.

I saw 24 Golden Box Cars being pulled by me each morning. Every morning, God gives you 24 Golden Hours. What you place in each of those 24 Golden Box Cars determines the speed and the distance your Train will move toward those next Cities of Achievement.

I noticed that I would often allow someone to come and sit in my office and "kill my time." They simply had nothing to do. I tried to be courteous and friendly by working quietly around them. Yet, they were filling up my hours with their idleness. My Golden Train was slowing down in the process.

If you do not decide the cargo of each of the 24 Golden Box Cars of each day, somebody else will decide the cargo and overload them. If someone else overloads your cars, your Golden Train will derail. Progress becomes impossible.

An Unproductive Day Is Always An Unhappy Day. You were created for increase. It is natural to increase and unnatural to decrease. So, every day you receive from God a fresh beginning. You can begin your life all over again.

Today is a *"mini*-life." It is a small, prototype of your *lifetime.*

If you failed today, do not get discouraged. Review it. Analyze it. What *missing* ingredients are obvious? What ingredients must be *added?* If you do not know the essential ingredients of a Perfect Day, you will never know the ingredients of a wonderful and glorious lifetime.

When a famous hamburger chain discovered how to make their store successful, they *duplicated* it. They made it happen hundreds of times throughout the earth. They did not begin *multiplying* until they had created a perfect store, a *prototype* of what they wanted to *multiply.*

Most of us have never discovered how to carefully sculpture even one wonderful and glorious day...The Perfect Day. "But the path of the just is as the shining light, that shineth more and more unto the perfect day" (Proverbs 4:18).

Your life should have a daily plan. "For which of you, intending to build a tower, sitteth not down first, and counteth the cost, whether he have sufficient to finish it? Lest haply, after he hath laid the foundation, and is not able to finish it, all that behold it begin to mock him, Saying, This man began to build, and was not able to finish" (Luke 14:28-30).

Nobody really knows your future except your Father. The Apostle Paul himself said, "And now, behold, I go bound in the spirit unto Jerusalem, not knowing the things that shall befall me there: Save that the Holy Ghost witnesseth in every city, saying that bonds and afflictions abide me" (Acts 20:22,23).

You must become time-conscious in spiritual matters. "To day if ye will hear His voice, harden not your hearts" (Hebrews 4:7).

You must encourage your love circle daily. These are those who are closest to you. "But exhort one another daily, while it is called to day; lest any of you be hardened through the deceitfulness of sin" (Hebrews 3:13).

One Discovery Can Birth A Lifetime Of Prosperity. Each day is a chance to create a perfect life. Your life *is* today. Every morning you will receive another opportunity to create The Perfect Day.

Your provision is a daily event. Jesus prayed this prayer, "Give us day by day our daily bread" (Luke 11:3).

You should mentor someone daily. Jesus did. "And He taught daily in the temple" (Luke 19:47).

You must daily pursue and accept mercy and forgiveness for any wrong. "It is of the Lord's mercies that we are not consumed, because His compassions fail not. They are new every morning: great is Thy faithfulness" (Lamentations 3:22,23).

Eternity is in you. You were created a pilgrim. You are on a journey. It never ends. You see, He is our Alpha and Omega, the beginning and the end. "Looking unto Jesus, the Author and Finisher of our faith;" (Hebrews 12:2). "For in Him we live, and move, and have our being;" (Acts 17:28).

You were created for movement. You are constantly moving toward Him, toward your Assignment, toward the dreams and goals He has planned for your life. Will you *arrive?*

Only when He is your destination.

Remember: *Your Assignment Is Actually An Hourly Event.*

Attitude Is Promoted Before Genius.

-MIKE MURDOCK

⇒ 21 ⇐

YOUR WILLINGNESS, NOT YOUR PERFECTION, WILL QUALIFY YOU FOR YOUR ASSIGNMENT.

Your Flaws Will Not Necessarily Disqualify You.

Your *attitude* can.

Your Assignment is perfect.

You are not. "For He knoweth our frame; He remembereth that we are dust" (Psalm 103:14).

Your goodness is not enough to qualify you for your Assignment. I wrote a song many years ago, "He Does Not Always Call The Qualified, But He Qualifies The Called." The Scripture says, "But we are all as an unclean thing, and all our righteousnesses are as filthy rags; and we all do fade as a leaf; and our iniquities, like the wind, have taken us away" (Isaiah 64:6).

The psalmist declared, "every man at his best state is altogether vanity" (Psalm 39:5).

Review the Heroes of Faith in Hebrews 11. Why are they celebrated? None of them are remembered for their lives of perfection, but rather for their *confidence* toward God. Their *faith* was magnetic and powerful.

They were *willing* to do anything God said.

Abraham lied. Twice! He told his wife, Sarai, "Say, I pray thee, thou art my sister: that it may be well with me for thy sake; and my soul shall live because of thee" (Genesis 12:13). "And Abraham said of Sarah his wife, She is my sister: and Abimelech king of Gerar sent, and took Sarah" (Genesis 20:2). Obviously, it was not his lifestyle nor pattern of life, but fear affected his integrity.

Jacob lied. He deceived his father, Isaac, to secure the

birthright from his older brother, Esau. His mother, Rebecca, cooperated with him. "And Jacob said unto his father, I am Esau thy firstborn; I have done according as thou badest me: arise, I pray thee, sit and eat of my venison, that thy soul may bless me" (Genesis 27:19). His sons then followed his habit of deception.

The sons of Jacob lied. What Jacob made happen for his father, his sons made happen for him in deceiving him regarding Joseph. Yet, Jacob continued to pursue God so intensely that God even changed his name!

Moses was a murderer. He became a fugitive from the law. He killed an Egyptian whom he saw beating a Hebrew worker. Fearful, he ran away to hide in the desert. His life was scarred, marred, and alienated from the very place where he was supposed to be a Deliverer (see Exodus 2:11-15). Yet, we see that God did not forget him. The angel appeared to him in a burning bush. God spoke to Moses and reminded him of his Assignment.

Your *worthiness* does not qualify you.

Your *willingness* to heal qualifies you.

Your abilities do not compel God to use you.

It is God's compassion toward those who need you. "And the Lord said, I have surely seen the affliction of my people which are in Egypt, and have heard their cry by reason of their taskmasters; for I know their sorrows; And I am come down to deliver them out of the hand of the Egyptians, and to bring them up out of that land unto a good land and a large, unto a land flowing with milk and honey;" (Exodus 3:7,8).

The pain of the captives causes God to give us an Assignment. The meekness and deep caring heart of Moses made him great. And this man, who was so stained by failure, became a close friend to God. "And the Lord spake unto Moses face to face, as a man speaketh unto his friend" (Exodus 33:11).

Samson visited harlots. He was often vulnerable and weak in the presence of alluring women. "Then went Samson to Gaza, and saw there an harlot, and went in unto her" (Judges 16:1). Yet, his ability to reach for God after failure qualified him to be among the Heroes of Faith in Hebrews (see Hebrews 11:32).

When satan has made a fool of you, repentance can create an exit from your failure.

David committed adultery. Then, he murdered Bathsheba's

husband, Uriah, to cover up his sin. Yet, the hand of God reached down again and brought healing and forgiveness. Yes, he paid the price. Judgment came. But his *willingness* to get up after failure qualified him to continue with his Assignment (read 2 Samuel 11).

Peter, the blustering fisherman, denied the Lord three times. When pressure came, he folded. "Then began he to curse and to swear, saying, I know not the man. And immediately the cock crew. And Peter remembered the word of Jesus, which said unto him, Before the cock crow, thou shalt deny Me thrice. And he went out, and wept bitterly" (Matthew 26:74,75). Those tears were the river that rushed him toward mercy and restoration.

Peter became so victorious through the mercy of Jesus that he was able to write later, "Wherein ye greatly rejoice, though now for a season, if need be, ye are in heaviness through manifold temptations: That the trial of your faith, being much more precious than of gold that perisheth, though it be tried with fire, might be found unto praise and honour and glory at the appearing of Jesus Christ: Whom having not seen, ye love; in Whom, though now ye see Him not, yet believing, ye rejoice with joy unspeakable and full of glory: Receiving the end of your faith, even the salvation of your souls" (1 Peter 1:6-9).

Have you failed God?

Have you failed those who love you?

Have you felt sick at heart because your conduct and behavior have been unbecoming to a child of God?

Do not quit. Do not stop reaching. Everything you have ever wanted is ahead of you, not behind you.

God Is Not Through Blessing You!

I wrote a song several years ago, "God's Not Through Blessing You." Here are some of those words:

♪ A man one day lost every dime to his name;
His best friends even said he was through;
God said to Job, your best days are just ahead;
'Cause I am not through blessing you.

God's not through blessing you;

God's not through blessing you;
Never give up, what He said He will do; ♪
God's not through blessing you. ♪

God is not through using you either.

Isaiah 1:19 declares, "If ye be willing and obedient, ye shall eat the good of the land:" Believe it.

Remember: *Your Willingness, Not Your Perfection, Will Qualify You For Your Assignment.*

❦ 22 ❦

YOUR INVESTMENT IN WISDOM REVEALS YOUR PASSION FOR YOUR ASSIGNMENT.

The Proof Of Desire Is Pursuit.

Wisdom is the greatest gift you can pursue.

It is the secret to uncommon achievement and uncommon greatness.

The Successful value the discoveries of others. I am always amused by those who declare, "there is no new thing under the sun" (Ecclesiastes 1:9). They are quoting a discouraged and disappointed man who pursued materialistic things during apostate seasons of his life.

Solomon did not exhaust the creativity of God on earth. When God rested on the seventh day, He did not stop having ideas and plans. He merely rested. After all, He is the One who promised, "Behold, I will do a new thing; now it shall spring forth; shall ye not know it? I will even make a way in the wilderness, and rivers in the desert" (Isaiah 43:19).

His mercies are even described as, "new every morning:" (Lamentations 3:23).

You are not born with all the Wisdom necessary for your Assignment. Others possess rare and unique gifts and revelations. Paul understood this. "For to one is given by the Spirit the word of Wisdom; to another the word of knowledge by the same Spirit; For as the body is one, and hath many members, and all the members of that one body, being many, are one body: so also is Christ" (1 Corinthians 12:8,12).

You need *others*.

You need their *knowledge*.

You need what God has *revealed* to them. "And the eye cannot say unto the hand, I have no need of thee: nor again the head to the feet, I have no need of you" (1 Corinthians 12:21).

8 Facts You Should Know About Wisdom

1. *Wisdom Is The Most Important Thing On Earth.* "Wisdom is the principal thing;" (Proverbs 4:7).

2. *You Must Pursue Wisdom.* It will not come to you. "Get Wisdom, get understanding:" (Proverbs 4:5).

3. *Wisdom Can Be Forgotten.* You must constantly read and study to keep yourself stirred and reminded. "...forget it not; neither decline from the words of my mouth" (Proverbs 4:5).

4. *You Can Know Wisdom And Deliberately Walk Away From It.* "Forsake her not," (Proverbs 4:6).

5. *Wisdom Will Preserve And Protect You If You Love And Pursue Her.* "She shall preserve thee: love her, and she shall keep thee" (Proverbs 4:6).

6. *Wisdom Is The Key To Every Promotion In Your Life.* "Exalt her, and she shall promote thee:" (Proverbs 4:8).

7. *Wisdom Brings You Honor, Credibility And Acceptance By Others.* "She shall bring thee to honour, when thou dost embrace her. She shall give to thine head an ornament of grace: a crown of glory shall she deliver to thee" (Proverbs 4:8,9).

8. *The Wisdom Imparted By God To Men Has Been Documented In Thousands Of Books.* It is accessible, reachable and just moments away. Think about it: You are reading this book today. Truths burned into my heart late at night in The Secret Place are now beginning to burn in your own heart, too. This is the power of a book. As I have often said, *God sent His Son, but He left His book.*

Books are feared by tyrants. One book can strip the power from a controlling dictator of a country. You have heard in this generation how a novel so incensed an entire nation that a price of millions of dollars was placed on the author's head. Why kill an author? His revelation, opinion or words potentially could strip leaders of their tyrannical power.

4 Facts About Reading

1. *The Most Uncommon Mentor To Ministers, Paul, Urged*

Personal Reading And Study. "Study to shew thyself approved unto God, a workman that needeth not to be ashamed, rightly dividing the Word of truth" (2 Timothy 2:15).

2. *Reading Wisdom Books Will Sustain The Revelation Planted Within You.* "But continue thou in the things which thou hast learned and hast been assured of, knowing of whom thou hast learned them; And that from a child thou hast known the holy scriptures, which are able to make thee wise unto salvation through faith which is in Christ Jesus" (2 Timothy 3:14,15).

3. *Reading The Word Of God Will Perfect Your Life.* "All scripture is given by inspiration of God, and is profitable for doctrine, for reproof, for correction, for instruction in righteousness: That the man of God may be perfect, throughly furnished unto all good works" (2 Timothy 3:16,17).

Picture Paul in prison. He is destitute. He has emptied his entire life. He has studied, preached and debated. He tells Timothy to bring his coat to him in prison. He is wet and cold. He needs an extra coat. How important are his books? He writes from the prison, "bring with thee...the books, but *especially the parchments*" (2 Timothy 4:13). Above everything else he wanted was his reading materials.

Learners Become Leaders.

Leaders Are Always Readers.

4. *Great Men Have Often Fasted Meals To Have Finances To Purchase Books.* You can spend $10 on a meal and be hungry four hours later. You can spend $10 on a book and have a *lifetime friend* that generates energy, enthusiasm and Wisdom for the rest of your life.

Several years ago, I purchased a book for $84. One book. My young Traveling Assistant was shocked.

"I cannot believe you would pay $84 for just one book!" he exclaimed.

"Oh, son, I really did not pay $84 for a book. I purchased a man's life for $84. I will learn within two hours what took him twenty years of living and research to learn. I would be a fool not to hand the man $84 for twenty years of research."

When people seriously debate the Wisdom of investing $20 in powerful and worthwhile books, I know their potential for success is virtually nonexistent. I have watched people pass by a life changing book saying, "I really cannot afford it." Then, watch them drive home in a $30,000 car arguing over how to pay their monthly car note.

Become informed.

Read everything you can about your Assignment.

Build the focus of your library around your Assignment. Most of your books should be linked to something God has told you to do with your life.

Recently, I walked into a home and saw a bookshelf full of books. "Oh, you love books! Have you read these books?"

"Not really," was the reply. "You see, I got them at a garage sale for $1.00." None of the books were connected to their Assignment. They simply bought books because they were inexpensive and looked good on the shelves.

Never buy a book simply because it is a bargain. Any unread book on your shelf may become emotionally burdensome. You may even feel guilty over an unread book. Refuse to collect unnecessary books.

16 Keys To Building Your Personal Wisdom Library

1. *Continuously Search For Books That Are Connected To Your Assignment.* You may find them in places you never dreamed. Used book stores often have great purchases for just a few dollars.

2. *Never Buy Retail When You Can Buy Wholesale.* Many books are being discounted in major stores if you will look for them when you go shopping.

3. *Ask Your Mentor Which Five Books He Would Recommend Most For Your Life.*

4. *Use A Pink Highlighter Pen Continuously When You Read To Mark The Pages That Matter The Most.* Mark up the book. It is your book for learning, not for display so others will be impressed.

5. *Read Credible Authors.* "And we beseech you, brethren, to know them which labour among you, and are over you in the Lord, and admonish you;" (1 Thessalonians 5:12).

6. *Read For A Purpose.* Read for discovery. There is a place for passive and relaxed leisurely reading. But, when you are

pursuing the Wisdom of God, extract from that book everything you possibly can.

7. *Set Aside A Portion Of Your Finances Specifically For Wisdom In Your Monthly Budget.* You have budgeted for electricity, food, clothes, insurance, housing and transportation. You will not be able to pay for any of it without Wisdom! Place Wisdom second on your budget list after the tithe.

8. *Take A Speed-Reading Course.* Invest the days and dollars to increase your speed reading skills. It has been a proven fact that those who read slowly experience wandering thoughts. The faster you read, the more you actually remember.

9. *Never Purchase A Book Without Reviewing It Thoroughly First.* I have spent money that I regretted because a book cover looked appealing. It promised more than it could deliver. Never purchase a book you have not reviewed.

10. *Never Loan Your Books To Others.* If someone wants to xerox a page from a reference manual, fine. They can do it on the spot. Do not let them take a book out of your home. Some of the most wonderful books I have ever owned were loaned to and lost by careless and lazy people who were too stingy to purchase their own.

11. *Establish A Separate Place Or Room As Your Personal "Wisdom Room."* (If it is a mere corner of a room, at least name it your "Wisdom Corner.")

12. *Establish A Specific Time Each Day When You Will Focus On Reading.* It may be for one hour or ten minutes, but the habit will become invaluable to your life.

13. *Keep A Microcassette Handy And Use It Daily.* Since you can talk six times faster than you can write, you will be able to gather data and file it in notebooks accordingly.

14. *Give Books As Gifts At Special Events, Holidays And Especially For Christmas Gifts.* Nothing lasts longer in the heart of another than Wisdom. Clothes are a matter of personal taste and preference. Gifts that enrich others are the gifts that are remembered. They are the gifts that truly make a lasting difference.

15. *Secure Membership Cards At Your Local Bookstore That Provide A Generous Discount.* Many bookstores today provide

discounts if you are a consistent customer of that store. It pays off in the long run.

16. *Keep Receipts On Every Book Purchase.* If the book is connected to your career and calling, it could be a tax deduction.

Remember: *Your Investment In Wisdom Reveals Your Passion For Your Assignment.*

RECOMMENDED BOOKS
BR-8 Wisdom Gift Catalog (48 pages)
For Your Free Copy Call 1-888-WISDOM-1 (1-888-947-3661)

～ 23 ～

YOUR RELATIONSHIPS CONTROL THE SUCCESS OF YOUR ASSIGNMENT.

You Cannot Succeed Alone.

That is why every relationship in your life should be defined and clearly understood.

18 Facts You Should Consider In Evaluating Your Relationships

1. *Your Friends Affect Your Future.* Each relationship in your life grows weeds or flowers.

2. *Each Relationship Feeds A Weakness Or A Strength.*

3. *Each Friendship Is Comfortable With Your Present Or Compatible With Your Future.*

4. *Every Relationship Is A Current That Sweeps You Toward Your Assignment Or Moves You Away From It.*

5. *Some Relationships Can Damage You Irreparably.* "And have no fellowship with the unfruitful works of darkness, but rather reprove them" (Ephesians 5:11).

6. *Some Relationships Multiply Your Wisdom.* "He that walketh with wise men shall be wise: but a companion of fools shall be destroyed" (Proverbs 13:20).

7. *The Purpose Of Wisdom Is To Disconnect You From Wrong People.* "For the Lord giveth wisdom: To deliver thee from the way of the evil man, To deliver thee from the strange woman," (Proverbs 2:6,12,16).

8. *Your Future Is Determined By The People You Permit Near You.*

9. *When Satan Wants To Destroy You, He Puts A Person In*

Your Life.

10. *When God Wants To Promote You, He Puts A Person In Your Life.*

11. *Those Who Are Fighting Against God Will Fight Against The God In You.*

12. *Those Who Despise God, Will Despise Your Obedience To God.*

13. *Those Who Desire God Will Recognize The God In You.*

14. *Those Who Do Not Increase You Will Inevitably Decrease You.*

15. *Those Who Do Not Make Deposits Eventually Make Withdrawals From You.* How do you discern a worthy relationship? By the Godly influence upon your Assignment.

16. *Each Friendship Will Abort Or Advance Your Assignment.*

17. *The Holy Spirit Alone Can Direct You To The Right People Who Will Assist You In Completing Your Assignment* (read Acts 8).

18. *No Relationship Is Ever Insignificant.*

You Will Need 5 Kinds Of Relationships To Succeed In Your Assignment

1. *Mentors*
2. *Protégés*
3. *Friends*
4. *Golden Connections*
5. *Enemies*

8 Facts You Should Know About Mentors

1. *Mentors Are Those Who Know What You Do Not Know And Who Have Gone Where You Want To Go.* Elijah was a Mentor to Elisha. Moses was a Mentor to Joshua. Naomi was a Mentor to Ruth. Mordecai was a Mentor to Esther. Paul was a Mentor to Timothy.

2. *Your Mentor Is Your Coach, Not Your Cheerleader.* Your Mentor does not always focus on your good qualities. He is there for correction and direction. God will use others to be cheerleaders.

3. *Your Mentor Does Not Need What You Know; You Need What Your Mentor Knows.*

4. *You Are Not Essential For The Success Of Your Mentor; But He Is Essential For Your Success.*

5. *Your Mentor Is A Serious Teacher That God Uses To Correct The Course Of Your Life.*

6. *God Will Use Various Mentors At Various Times And Seasons Of Your Life.*

7. *Mentorship Is A Relationship With Someone Who Treasures Your Success Above Your Approval Of Them.*

8. *Your Mentor Will Risk Alienation In Order To Produce Your Success.*

7 Facts You Should Know About Protégés

1. *Protégés Are Those Who Will Experience Their Greatest Discoveries While With You.*

2. *Your Children Should Become Your Protégés.*

3. *There Are Various Types Of Protégés, Just Like There Are Different Types Of Mentors.*

4. *There Are Productive Protégés And There Are Parasite Protégés.*

5. *The Uncommon Protégé Is The Student Who Receives You Continuously, Persistently And Thankfully.*

6. *The Uncommon Protégé Listens, Obeys And Completes Your Instructions.* Ruth obeyed Naomi and reached for Boaz. Esther obeyed Mordecai and approached the king. Elisha respected Elijah and followed him for the double portion.

7. *A Parasite Protégé Reaches For You Only During Crisis, Loss Or Lack.* They will not necessarily follow your instructions consistently. They simply want promotion, not correction. They only associate to gain credibility through the influence of the Mentor.

7 Facts You Should Know About Friends

1. *A Friend Is The Greatest Gift God Can Give You Other Than Himself.*

2. *Your Friend Will Stay Loyal During Crisis.*

3. *Your Friend Will Be Consistent During Upheavals.*

4. *Your Friend Will Be Truthful When It Hurts.*

5. *Your Friend Is Always Accessible During Your Times Of Loneliness.*

"A friend loveth at all times, and a brother is born for adversity" (Proverbs 17:17).

"Be not deceived: evil communications corrupt good manners" (1 Corinthians 15:33).

6. *Friendship Begins As A Seed.* It requires constant watering, nurturing and protection.

7. *A True Friend Will Increase Your Strength During Adversity.* "Two are better than one; and a threefold cord is not quickly broken" (Ecclesiastes 4:9,12).

4 Facts To Remember About Golden Connections

1. *Golden Connections Are Divine Bridges That Enable You To Exit From One Season And Enter Into Your Next Season Of Blessing.* The butler was a connection for Joseph to personally meet Pharaoh and interpret his dream. (See Chapter 17 for 14 Wisdom Keys you should know about the Golden Connection in your life.)

2. *The Briefest Encounter In Your Life Can Be A Golden Link To The Greatest Dreams You Have Carried In Your Lifetime.*

3. *Never Treat An Encounter Lightly Since God May Use It As A Golden Connection.*

4. *God Will Move You From The Pit Into The Palace Throughout The Days Of Your Assignment...Through Golden Connections.*

Joseph discovered it. The distance from the Pit to the Palace may only be *one* person away.

Always remember, no relationship is insignificant in your life.

Remember: *Your Relationships Will Determine The Success Of Your Assignment.*

❧ 24 ❧

IT IS YOUR PERSONAL RESPONSIBILITY TO INSPIRE OTHERS TO ASSIST YOU IN YOUR ASSIGNMENT.

————————⟫●⟪————————

You Will Always Need Others.

God arranged it so. You will need information, motivation and correction throughout every season.

10 Facts You Should Know About The Law Of Asking

1. *You Must Ask For Help.* "And I say unto you, Ask, and it shall be given you; seek, and ye shall find; knock, and it shall be opened unto you. For every one that asketh receiveth; and he that seeketh findeth; and to him that knocketh it shall be opened" (Luke 11:9,10).

2. *You Must Ask Mentors For Counsel.* They see what you do not see. They hear what you do not hear. They have been where you have not been.

Mentors *will not* respond to your *need*.

Mentors *will* respond to your *pursuit*.

Let me explain. The Holy Spirit observes you making mistakes every day. But, He does not always correct you unless you approach Him. You must reach. You must ask, seek and knock.

You must overcome your pride and reach for assistance. I watched a young protégé make a mistake a few weeks ago. I had a desire to mention it to him. But, he did not want conversation, analysis, or correction. I knew it. As I attempted to discuss it, he did not have time to hear my observations. So, I waited until he tasted the pain of his error. Then, he *reached.* I responded by reviewing his mistake and offering a solution.

3.   *Sinners Cannot Even Be Changed Unless They Ask Jesus To Help Them.* "Come unto Me, all ye that labour and are heavy laden, and I will give you rest. Take My yoke upon you, and learn of Me; for I am meek and lowly in heart: and ye shall find rest unto your souls. For My yoke is easy, and My burden is light" (Matthew 11:28-30).

4.   *Jesus Required That The Samaritan Woman Ask.* "Jesus answered and said unto her, If thou knewest the gift of God, and Who it is that saith to thee, Give Me to drink; thou wouldest have asked of Him, and He would have given thee living water" (John 4:10). Notice this important principle. She had a need. But He could not meet that need until she pursued, reached and *asked.* It is a Law of Life.

Pride keeps us from *reaching.*

5.   *The Proof Of Humility Is The Willingness To Reach.*

I failed to grasp this Law of Asking in my early ministry. I was too proud to call a pastor and say, "I am a young evangelist. I really believe I have a message that would bless your people and inspire your church. Would you give me the privilege of coming and sharing one night with your people?" I missed a thousand opportunities because of it.

Pride is a *thief* of blessings and relationships. I was too fearful to ask partners to support my ministry with monthly Seed. I wanted approval like many young evangelists. A major pastor of a large congregation once warned me, "I hope you never ask for financial help in your newsletter." I became fearful. I knew that doors would close if ministers were unhappy with my asking friends to sow into my ministry.

I was too inexperienced to grasp that he was asking for financial support from his people three times a week! Yet, it was "wrong" for me to ask for help in my newsletter to my partners once each month!

Several years of powerful ministry were lost. I could have been on radio and television, but I was afraid to ask for financial help.

It was a wonderful and glorious day of my life when three men sat in my living room in Houston, Texas, and interrogated me. "Are you doing everything you want to do for God at this point in your ministry?"

"No, of course not," I replied.

"Well, why is your ministry not on television and radio every week reaching the thousands with the gospel?" they asked rather aggressively.

"I do not have any money to pay for the television time," was my frustrated reply.

"Then, you must have *partners*, people whom the Lord calls along side you to hold up your hands in battle like Aaron and Hur held the hands of Moses."

Something turned on within me. I knew they were speaking truth to my heart. I just dreaded the potential alienation from certain ministers who would criticize me.

6. *You Have No Right To Anything You Have Not Pursued.* You can complain. You can gripe. You can become angry. But You Will Never Possess What You Are Unwilling To Pursue.

7. *You Must Learn To Ask Of God.* Ask Him for the tools and the resources you need to complete your Assignment.

8. *Ask God For Wisdom To Carry Out His Instructions Faithfully.* "If any of you lack wisdom, let him ask of God, that giveth to all men liberally, and upbraideth not; and it shall be given him" (James 1:5).

9. *Ask With Great Expectation For Answers To Prayer.* "But let him ask in faith, nothing wavering. For he that wavereth is like a wave of the sea driven with the wind and tossed. For let not that man think that he shall receive any thing of the Lord. A double minded man is unstable in all his ways" (James 1:6-8).

10. *Ask God To Direct People To Participate In Your Assignment.* "Pray ye therefore the Lord of the harvest, that He will send forth labourers into His harvest" (Matthew 9:38).

▶ Champions reach. Losers withdraw.

▶ Champions network. Losers disconnect.

▶ Reaching is *not* a sign of weakness.

▶ Reaching is a sign of *awareness*.

The Hebrew writer penned powerful instructions, "But to do good and to communicate forget not:" (Hebrews 13:16).

6 Keys To Developing Communication Skills

1. *Develop Your Speaking Skills.* Attend any class that helps you to become articulate.

2. *Make Every Conversation Count.*

3. *Cultivate Conscienceness And Clarity When Talking To Others.*

4. *Review Your Dictionary Continually.*

5. *Learn New Words Regularly.*

6. *Sculpture Every Sentence In Every Conversation.*

Remember: *It Is Your Personal Responsibility To Inspire Others To Assist You In Your Assignment.*

~ 25 ~

THE SUCCESS OF YOUR ASSIGNMENT MAY REQUIRE AN ABILITY TO NEGOTIATE EFFECTIVELY WITH OTHERS.

Negotiation Begins At Birth.

When babies cry, they are negotiating for attention. Teenagers constantly negotiate with parents. Husbands and wives negotiate continuously. One dictionary says that negotiation is "to discuss with a view to reaching an agreement."

Everyone will require a measure of negotiation in their pursuit of something that really matters to them. Obviously, the levels of desire vary. The integrity of others will vary.

Some will *lie* to achieve their goal.

Some will *steal* to achieve their goal.

Some will *kill* to achieve their goal.

Some will *terminate* your friendship to achieve something else they desire.

Some will *risk their own health* to achieve something they want.

Some will risk their entire *fortune* to achieve something they desire.

Some parents will forfeit the love of their children to achieve a goal.

Some children will walk away from their parents forever to achieve a temporary goal.

You will be continuously drawn to the negotiating table throughout your lifetime. It is like a magnet.

You cannot control the *desires* of others.

You cannot control the *behavior* of others.

You cannot *predict the price* another will pay at the negotiating table.

Negotiation is the ability to change the opinions of others through a climate of favor, instead of force. The decisions of others affect your circumstances. The city council determines the zoning of your land, whether it is residential or commercial. The salesman decides whether you purchase the car at his price or your price.

Your Assignment will always involve negotiating with others. They will have different viewpoints, experiences and needs. Their needs will generally matter far more to them than your needs.

You cannot avoid the negotiating table. Almost every decision you make will involve others at some level. It will affect those you love financially, emotionally, physically or even spiritually.

Uncommon negotiation occurs when you get what you desire by helping someone else get what they desire.

The Apostle Paul was a master negotiator. Educated in law, skilled in debate, and known for persuasion and logic, his writings are marvelous studies.

Pilate did not intimidate him.

Prestige did not intrigue him.

Wealth did not beckon to him.

Yet, when he spoke, kings listened and trembled.

Leadership sought him out.

His adversaries listened raptly and with great attentiveness to his viewpoints.

He knew when to be gentle, and when to be firm.

He knew when to listen, and when to speak.

He knew what to pursue, and what to avoid.

He knew a Master Key, Negotiation. His success was greatly affected by these negotiating skills.

Negotiation gifts can be developed with your family. It starts in your childhood.

Your family is the *testing ground* for your future. It may be good or it may be bad. But, your family is a gift from God to help you become qualified for enemy territory.

If you do not learn to negotiate effectively with your family, you will not negotiate effectively with your enemies.

If you learn the secrets of effective negotiation with those you love, it will inevitably affect your negotiation experiences with others in your future.

That is why the Bible has been given to us. It gives us the secrets, principles, and laws of negotiating with others.

It reveals how children are to conduct themselves toward their parents.

It is also true that many parents mistreat their children (see Ephesians 6:4).

The most important truth you will ever learn in negotiating with others is to *listen for the inner voice of the Holy Spirit.* Whether you are in the presence of a serious enemy or your best friend, listen to the voice of the Holy Spirit regarding them. Jesus instructed His disciples to depend on the Holy Spirit in these times: "And when they bring you unto the synagogues, and unto magistrates, and powers, take ye no thought how or what thing ye shall answer, or what ye shall say: For the Holy Ghost shall teach you in the same hour what ye ought to say" (Luke 12:11,12).

4 Powerful Principles In The Negotiating World Of The Christian

1. *God Anticipated Difficult Situations Where Negotiation Would Be Necessary.*

2. *God Wants You To Be Relaxed And Unworried, But Aware That The Holy Spirit Is Present In These Scenarios Of Negotiation.*

3. *God Desires That You Become A Learner, One Who Is Willing To Be Taught And Mentored By The Holy Spirit In Such Situations.*

4. *God Wants You To Trust Him For The Outcome.*

20 Powerful Keys To Effective Negotiation

1. *Never Fear What Others Can Do To You.* "For God hath not given us the spirit of fear; but of power, and of love, and of a sound mind" (2 Timothy 1:7). "In God have I put my trust: I will not be afraid what man can do unto me" (Psalm 56:11).

2. *Concentrate On How Much Good You Can Do For The Other Person With Whom You Are Negotiating.* "Withhold not good from them to whom it is due, when it is in the power of thine hand to do it" (Proverbs 3:27).

3. *Expect God To Reward You For The Good You Do, Not The Person With Whom You Are Negotiating.* "Knowing that whatsoever good thing any man doeth, the same shall he receive of the Lord, whether he be bond or free" (Ephesians 6:8).

4. *Speak Nothing That Does Not Edify And Strengthen Those At The Negotiating Table.* "Let no corrupt communication proceed out of your mouth, but that which is good to the use of edifying, that it may minister grace unto the hearers" (Ephesians 4:29).

5. *Stifle Any Anger That Threatens To Enter The Negotiations.* "Let all bitterness, and wrath, and anger, and clamour, and evil speaking, be put away from you, with all malice: And be ye kind one to another, tenderhearted, forgiving one another, even as God for Christ's sake hath forgiven you" (Ephesians 4:31,32).

6. *Avoid Any Attempt By Others To Make The Atmosphere Become Foolish, Lighthearted Or Jesting.* "Neither filthiness, nor foolish talking, nor jesting, which are not convenient: but rather giving of thanks" (Ephesians 5:4).

7. *Stay Alert To Any Attempt To Deceive You At The Negotiating Table.* "Let no man deceive you with vain words:" (Ephesians 5:6).

8. *Do Not Enter Into Any Bond, Covenant, Or Contract With The Enemies Of God.* "And have no fellowship with the unfruitful works of darkness, but rather reprove them" (Ephesians 5:11).

9. *Permit The Tool Of Time To Sculpture An Acceptable Agreement With Others.* "The Lord is good unto them that wait for Him, to the soul that seeketh Him" (Lamentations 3:25).

10. *Expect The Ability And Wisdom Of God To Compensate For Your Personal Weaknesses, Limitations And Fears.* "And I was with you in weakness, and in fear, and in much trembling. And my speech and my preaching was not with enticing words of man's wisdom, but in demonstration of the Spirit and of power: That your faith should not stand in the wisdom of men, but in the power of God" (1 Corinthians 2:3-5).

11. *Develop The Ability To Listen Carefully To Every Word Spoken.* "A wise man will hear, and will increase learning;" (Proverbs 1:5). Listen to what is *not* spoken as well as words spoken. Listen for *attitudes.* Listen for areas of *pain* in others.

12. *Do Not Make Any Decision Without Sufficient*

Information. "He that answereth a matter before he heareth it, it is folly and shame unto him" (Proverbs 18:13).

13. *Remember The Power Of Silence.* "Even a fool, when he holdeth his peace, is counted wise: and he that shutteth his lips is esteemed a man of understanding" (Proverbs 17:28).

14. *Refuse To Accept Any Gift That Could Possibly Influence The Negotiations Unwisely.* "A wicked man taketh a gift out of the bosom to pervert the ways of judgment" (Proverbs 17:23).

15. *Stay Cheerful Through The Negotiation.* "A merry heart doeth good like a medicine: but a broken spirit drieth the bones" (Proverbs 17:22). God will not let you fail.

16. *Do Not Share Everything You Know At The Negotiation Table.* "He that hath knowledge spareth his words:" (Proverbs 17:27).

17. *Keep A Congenial But Focused Attitude Throughout The Negotiations.* "A man that hath friends must shew himself friendly:" (Proverbs 18:24).

18. *Define Clearly Everything You Expect During The Negotiations.* "Ask, and it shall be given you: seek, and ye shall find; knock, and it shall be opened unto you:" (Matthew 7:7). You have nothing to lose by asking. The worst thing that could happen when you ask someone for something is that they could reject you. If you fail to pursue something you really desire, you will live the remainder of your life wondering "what could have been."

19. *Listen Carefully To Hear What Is Loudest In The Mind Of Another.* When Abigail sent her employees to ward off David's assault on Nabal, her husband, she brought him food. Why? It was the focus of David. You must hear what another person is hearing *inside their mind.* You must listen carefully to what is *loudest* inside of them (read 1 Samuel 25).

20. *Make Certain You Understand Completely What Their Expectations Are From The Negotiations.* They have needs. Some may be overwhelming to them. Do you know what these needs are? Do you know what they cannot give up?

You, too, must not forget this powerful principle: *The Success Of Your Assignment May Require An Ability To Negotiate Effectively With Others.*

One Day Of Favor
Is Worth
A Lifetime Of Labor.

-MIKE MURDOCK

❧ 26 ❧

YOUR ASSIGNMENT MAY OFTEN REQUIRE UNCOMMON FAVOR WITH SOMEONE.

━━━━━━━━━⟫●⟪━━━━━━━━━

One Day Of Favor Is Worth A Lifetime Of Labor.
Examine the life of Joseph. Year after year, he struggled for recognition from his brothers and father concerning his dream. The result? He was sold into Egypt as a slave to a passing caravan of Ishmaelites. He worked his way up in the house of Potiphar, a government official.

That is favor.
Suddenly, he experienced a horrible and terrifying chapter of false accusation. The wife of Potiphar attempted to seduce him. But he stayed true to God *and* Potiphar.

She accused him of attempted rape. He was thrust into the dungeon. He needed another current of favor. He became a model prisoner. Eventually they placed him in charge of the other prisoners. His trustworthiness had emerged, as always. He then interpreted a dream for the butler. Two years later Pharaoh called for him, and the currents of favor flowed again. Within 24 hours, Joseph went from the prison into the palace.

17 Facts You Should Know About Favor

1. *Favor Will Bring You To Places Money Cannot Buy.* Joseph was a prisoner, not a millionaire. Yet, the favor of God brought him to the palace.

2. *Favor Produces Miracles You Cannot Perform.* The woman with the issue of blood for 12 years had no money. But, the favor of God linked her with Jesus. Her healing was immediate when she touched His robe.

3. *Favor Links You To Promotions For Which You Have Not Labored.* Joseph became Prime Minister in a day...because of the favor with Pharoah. One dream. One day. It produced a lifetime promotion.

4. *Favor Is Promised To The Obedient And Godly.* "For Thou, Lord, wilt bless the righteous; with favour wilt Thou compass him as with a shield" (Psalm 5:12).

5. *Favor Can Increase In Waves In Your Life.* "And Jesus increased in wisdom and stature, and in favour with God and man" (Luke 2:52). "Thou hast granted me life and favour, and Thy visitation hath preserved my spirit" (Job 10:12).

6. *When You Increase In Wisdom, You Will Increase In Favor With God And Man.* "And Jesus increased in wisdom and stature, and in favour with God and man" (Luke 2:52).

7. *It Is Appropriate To Acknowledge And Pursue Favor.* Ruth did so with Boaz. "Then she said, Let me find favour in thy sight, my lord; for that thou hast comforted me, and for that thou hast spoken friendly unto thine handmaid, though I be not like unto one of thine handmaidens" (Ruth 2:13).

8. *Favor Is The Essential Ingredient That Turns A Crisis Into A Miracle.* "And it was so, when the king saw Esther the queen standing in the court, that she obtained favour in his sight: and the king held out to Esther the golden sceptre that was in his hand. So Esther drew near, and touched the top of the sceptre" (Esther 5:2). It was unlawful for Esther to approach the king when he had not called for her. It was a crucial and very critical time. She could have been put to death. Favor was the difference between death and life.

9. *Your Personal Integrity Influences The Flow Of Favor Toward You.* "Let not mercy and truth forsake thee: bind them about thy neck; write them upon the table of thine heart: So shalt thou find favour and good understanding in the sight of God and man" (Proverbs 3:3,4).

10. *Doing Your Job Well Generates Favor Toward You From A Boss.* "Good understanding giveth favour:" (Proverbs 13:15). Diligence positions you with great men.

11. *Favor Causes The Dormant Potential Greatness Within You To Blossom And Flourish.* Just as rain causes the crops of Harvest time to flourish, favor from others unlocks greatness which

is hidden in you. "In the light of the king's countenance is life; and his favour is as a cloud of the latter rain" (Proverbs 16:15).

12. *Favor Will Take You Further Than Money.* "A good name is rather to be chosen than great riches, and loving favour rather than silver and gold" (Proverbs 22:1).

13. *Favor Births Increase And Multiplication.* When the disciples broke bread together, when they had fellowship and walked in joy praising God, favor flowed. The Lord added to the church daily while His favor flowed. It appears that *increase* follows favor. "Praising God, and having favour with all the people. And the Lord added to the church daily such as should be saved" (Acts 2:47).

14. *Favor Turns Enemies Into Friends.* Someone is going to be good to you today! Expect it.

15. *It Takes More Than Your Gifts, Talents And Skills To Generate The Flow Of Favor.*

16. *Favor Requires God.*

Joseph was probably not the first person to interpret a dream for Pharaoh. He had people in the palace who did it for a living. But, he was the first man ever promoted to the number two position in the kingdom. *That is favor.*

Ruth was probably not the first widow Boaz ever saw gleaning in his fields. But she was the one he married. *That is favor.*

I depend completely on the favor of God in my life on a daily basis. He is the Source of everything I possess today. I do not have a thing He did not give to me.

Do you need uncommon favor today? Are you *sowing* uncommon favor toward others today? Have you started sowing favor into your mother and father? Have you honored your pastor and those in spiritual authority with significant favor?

When you want a Harvest of Favor, you must sow the Seeds of Favor.

17. *Favor Is Different Than "Favors."* Favors, are often actions designed to influence, control and manipulate others. This is deceptive. It is the satanic substitute for the Law of Divine Favor. You see, politicians do "favors" for businessmen. You have seen it happen many times in the business world. Someone agrees to cooperate in a business deal, if they will *exchange* advantages. These favors are actions that create a *Network of Obligation,* just

like spider webs, to keep you indebted to someone.

Is anything wrong with this? Yes.

▶ You will eventually despise those who obligate you.

▶ You will always be uncomfortable in the presence of someone you *owe.*

So, move away from those who say after a meal, "I will owe you one." Or, "Do not forget now, you owe me a favor." Run for your life from those who tabulate the favors they do for you.

I am talking about something *much different.*

Favor is the attitude of *giving* to another.

Favors are the acts of *exchanging* for an anticipated advantage returned.

When you sow favor, do not obligate others to produce something in return for you. That is a business transaction. That is *not* Favor. That is an exchange.

Favor is when you sow into the life of another, knowing that the Lord of the Harvest will repay you, not necessarily the person receiving from you.

▶ God is your Source.

▶ God determines the schedule He has for your Harvest to arrive.

▶ God is more capable of rewarding you than anyone.

9 Important Keys In Developing The Miracle Of Favor In Your Daily Life

1. *You Must First Solve A Problem For Someone.* Favor occurs when you lift the burden off another. Joseph was trustworthy. He removed the stress of daily business from the mind of Potiphar. Favor flowed.

When Paul prayed, he saw the healing of the father of Publius on the island of Melita. Later, he wrote that the people, "also honoured us with many honours; and when we departed, they laded us with such things as were necessary" (Acts 28:10).

When Joseph interpreted the perplexing dream of Pharaoh, promotion followed (see Genesis 41:37-45). The first thirty years of the life of Joseph were tumultuous, stormy and violent. At the age of thirty, he became second in command of all of Egypt. Favor can bring you from sorrow to ecstasy within 24 hours.

2. *You Must Sow Favor To Create Favor.* Joseph sowed favor toward Potiphar by protecting his marriage from infidelity. God honored this.

Mordecai revealed an assassination plot against the king, and favor flowed. He sowed favor by protecting the life of the king.

Ruth labored daily to provide for her mother-in-law, Naomi. God sent Boaz to her to provide for her. Oh, believe me today! The greatest Wisdom Key that has affected my daily provision and blessing of life has been this: "What You Make Happen For Others, God Will Make Happen For You."

3. *Start Showing Favor To Everyone Close To You.* "Withhold not good from them to whom it is due, when it is in the power of thine hand to do it" (Proverbs 3:27).

4. *Sow Words Of Love And Kindness Continuously To Those Around You.* "Death and life are in the power of the tongue: and they that love it shall eat the fruit thereof" (Proverbs 18:21).

5. *Stay In The Center Of Your Expertise, And Use Your Greatest Gifts.* "A man's gift maketh room for him, and bringeth him before great men" (Proverbs 18:16).

6. *When Possible, Sow Gifts Of Love Into The Lives Of Others.* "Every man is a friend to him that giveth gifts" (Proverbs 19:6).

7. *Move Swiftly To Complete An Instruction From Your Boss.* "Seest thou a man diligent in his business? he shall stand before kings; he shall not stand before mean men" (Proverbs 22:29).

8. *Respect The Rules Of Protocol, The Expected And Desired Standards Of Conduct.* Egyptians hated beards. So, "Then Pharaoh sent and called Joseph, and they brought him hastily out of the dungeon: and he shaved himself, and changed his raiment, and came in unto Pharaoh" (Genesis 41:14).

It is interesting that even table etiquette is referred to in Scripture. "When thou sittest to eat with a ruler, consider diligently what is before thee: And put a knife to thy throat, if thou be a man given to appetite" (Proverbs 23:1,2).

9. *Expect Favor Every Day Of Your Life.* "But without faith it is impossible to please Him: for he that cometh to God must believe that He is, and that He is a rewarder of them that diligently seek Him" (Hebrews 11:6).

Expectation is confidence. Confidence is a current that is sensed, felt and known. You can walk into a room and feel anger, love or confusion. So, when you *expect* the currents of favor to flow toward you, for some unexplainable and wonderful reason, *it happens.*

Wake up each day expecting new friends to be brought into your life.

Study the Law of Divine Favor throughout the Word of God.

Remember: *Your Assignment May Often Require Uncommon Favor With Someone.*

RECOMMENDED BOOKS AND TAPES
B-99   Secrets Of The Richest Man Who Ever Lived (177 pages/$10)
TS-89 School Of Wisdom, Vol. 4/Unleashing Uncommon Favor (6 tapes/$30)

➣ 27 ➣

GOD WILL NEVER PROMOTE YOU UNTIL YOU BECOME OVERQUALIFIED FOR YOUR PRESENT ASSIGNMENT.

————————

Your Assignment Can Change.

However, you must *become* qualified for your next season. Ruth wanted to live with Naomi. She had to qualify. Her tenacity and ability to give total focus to Naomi qualified her to move from Moab to Bethlehem.

One day, she wanted to marry Boaz. What qualified her to marry one of the wealthiest men in the city? She had carefully built a reputation of integrity and compassion. Everyone knew of her attitude toward Naomi.

She *became* qualified for Boaz.

The Secret Passage of Promotion for Daniel was the lion's den. It was the exit from Daniel's present, the gateway to his next season.

The Secret Passage of Promotion for the three Hebrew children was the fiery furnace. The three Hebrew children embraced the fiery furnace as an exit from their present and a gate into the next season.

The Secret Passage of Promotion for Joseph was false accusation. Joseph excelled in the prison after it. It was really his gate to significance.

5 Qualities That Affect Your Promotion

1. *Excellence.* "Whatsoever thy hand findeth to do, do it with thy might;" (Ecclesiastes 9:10).

2. *Problem Solving.* You must solve the problems that matter the most to your boss. "Withhold not good from them to whom it is due, when it is in the power of thine hand to do it" (Proverbs 3:27).

3. *Diligence.* Diligence is speedy attention to an assigned task. "He becometh poor that dealeth with a slack hand: but the hand of the diligent maketh rich" (Proverbs 10:4). "The soul of the sluggard desireth, and hath nothing: but the soul of the diligent shall be made fat" (Proverbs 13:4).

4. *Favor.* Especially with those in authority. Favor occurs when an instruction has been followed accurately and quickly. "Seest thou a man diligent in his business? he shall stand before kings; he shall not stand before mean men" (Proverbs 22:29).

5. *Cooperation.* Cooperation is getting along with others. The cause of strife is always known by others in an office. "Follow peace with all men, and holiness, without which no man shall see the Lord:" (Hebrews 12:14). "But foolish and unlearned questions avoid, knowing that they do gender strifes. And the servant of the Lord must not strive; but be gentle unto all men, apt to teach, patient," (2 Timothy 2:23,24).

One of the wealthiest men in America wrote an interesting article. When he sees a resumé of anyone who has difficulty in getting along with those around him, he refuses to hire the person. Their knowledge does not help. Their genius does not solve their lack of cooperation.

▶ *Survival* involves solving *your own* problems.

▶ *Promotion* involves solving the problems of *others.*

Promotion depends on the problems you are willing to solve for those around you. After Jesus addressed Peter regarding satan's desire to sift him as wheat, He gave him an instruction. It is fascinating. "But I have prayed for thee, that thy faith fail not: and when thou art converted, *strengthen thy brethren*" (Luke 22:32). Oh, my precious friend, please see this powerful principle!

An interesting experience occurred several years ago. I walked into my office after a 2,000 mile flight. I was weary and tired. A young lady who worked for me said, "May I talk to you?"

"How can I help you?"

"I need a raise," she declared emphatically.

"What do you want your raise to be?"

"I want you to pay me $1,000 a month more than what you have been paying me."

"Why?" was my puzzled and surprised reply.

"My husband and I are buying a new house and I need the money to make the payments," was her explanation.

I carefully explained to her that her salary was based on the *kind of problems* she solved. I asked her to bring me a list of the problems that she was currently solving linked to her present salary.

"When you want increased rewards, you must define your increased responsibilities," I explained. "You are paid relative to the problems you solve for someone. The janitor may receive $12 an hour while the attorney receives $150 each hour. Their salary is not based on their personal worth, but rather on the worth of the *problem they have selected to solve* with their time, energy and knowledge. If you want me to increase your salary, you must bring me a list of new problems you will begin to solve for me."

Obviously, this had never crossed her mind. In fact, she was not completing her *present* tasks in a timely fashion each week. She required continuous motivation from me. I had become her memo pad. She continuously forgot instructions. She required constant reminding. Her departure was not a painful experience for me whatsoever.

Even God will not promote the unqualified.

Do you want your boss to promote you?

Your *responsibilities* will increase.

Your *mistakes* become more costly.

Your *work* will be analyzed and scrutinized. "For unto whomsoever much is given, of him shall be much required: and to whom men have committed much, of him they will ask the more" (Luke 12:48).

Many employees desire equal pay with their boss. Yet, they rush out of the office the moment the clock turns 5:01 every afternoon. Their boss puts in 18 hour days. Their boss studies, reads and carefully builds his future.

You must *qualify* for the future you are desiring.

Remember: *God Will Never Promote You Until You Become Overqualified For Your Present Assignment.*

God Never Calls
The Qualified-
He Simply Qualifies
The Called.

-MIKE MURDOCK

∾ 28 ∾

YOUR ASSIGNMENT MAY EXPOSE YOUR PERSONAL LIMITATIONS TO REVEAL THE POWER OF GOD.

Your Assignment Is Bigger Than You Are.

When you have reached the end of yourself and exhausted your abilities, it is only *there* that the power of God becomes evident to you. This explains why He gives instructions that often leave you feeling helpless, vulnerable and even unprepared for an enemy or adversary.

Gideon felt his limitations. God reduced Gideon's army to 300 men just to reveal His divine ability and power. "So Gideon, and the hundred men that were with him, came unto the outside of the camp in the beginning of the middle watch; and they had but newly set the watch: and they blew the trumpets, and brake the pitchers that were in their hands. And the three companies blew the trumpets, and brake the pitchers, and held the lamps in their left hands, and the trumpets in their right hands to blow withal: and they cried, The sword of the Lord, and of Gideon. And they stood every man in his place round about the camp: and all the host ran, and cried, and fled. And the three hundred blew the trumpets, and the host fled" (Judges 7:19-23).

Moses felt his personal limitations. Moses felt incompetent, inarticulate and unintelligent when faced with his Assignment. "And Moses said unto the Lord, O my Lord, I am not eloquent, neither heretofore, nor since Thou hast spoken unto Thy servant: but I am slow of speech, and of a slow tongue" (Exodus 4:10).

It is only when you recognize your limitations, weaknesses and vulnerabilities, that God can show His arm strong toward you.

God requires *dependency*.

The wise respond, and become *addicted* to His presence.

David felt his personal limitations. David developed a total dependency on God. He had not proven the armor of Saul. "And David girded his sword upon his armour, and he assayed to go; for he had not proved it. And David said unto Saul, I cannot go with these; for I have not proved them. And David put them off him" (1 Samuel 17:39).

But, David knew God could use a slingshot.

He moved toward his Assignment with full *dependency* upon the Lord.

David declared it to Goliath. "Then said David to the Philistine, Thou comest to me with a sword, and with a spear, and with a shield: but I come to thee in the name of the Lord of hosts, the God of the armies of Israel, Whom thou hast defied. This day will the Lord deliver thee into mine hand; and I will smite thee, and take thine head from thee; that all the earth may know that there is a God in Israel...for the battle is the Lord's, and He will give you into our hands" (1 Samuel 17:45-47).

Oh, please grasp this principle! God is determined to reveal His power to His children. When He gives you an Assignment, it will take you to the edge of your strength *where your weaknesses are fully exposed.*

It will exhaust the best in you.

It will *require* God.

Never shrink your dreams to fit your present capabilities. God does not want you to live within the realm of your own competence. His joy is to watch you move in the supernatural, fully dependent upon His love and His power in every crisis toward the completion of your Assignment.

Plan on miracles.

Your Assignment will require them.

God is not dependent upon your *gifts*.

God is not dependent upon your *knowledge*.

God is not dependent upon your *experience*.

God is not dependent upon your *friendships*.

God merely wants you fully dependent upon Him. "Not that

we are sufficient of ourselves to think any thing as of ourselves; but our sufficiency *is* of God;" (2 Corinthians 3:5).

Remember: *Your Assignment May Expose Your Personal Limitations To Reveal The Power Of God.*

Those Who
  Transfer Knowledge
Are Also Capable
  Of Transferring Error.

-MIKE MURDOCK

≫ 29 ≫

WRONG MENTORSHIP CAN PARALYZE YOUR PROGRESS TOWARD YOUR ASSIGNMENT.

Error Is Devastating.

One small Seed of error can destroy the lifelong ministry of a godly man. I saw it happen more than 20 years ago in a small southern town. One of the leading ministers received favor, loyalty and respect from the entire town. I ministered for this precious man of God. He was admired and pursued.

His brother-in-law was an articulate and brilliant young man with unusual knowledge of Biblical languages. The brother-in-law was cynical, sarcastic, quarrelsome and continuously sowed discord regarding the doctrine of predestination. He believed that God pre-determined those who were saved or lost. You were either chosen or not. Your will had nothing to do with your eternal salvation. His militant stance on it wreaked havoc in the church of this pastor.

Obviously, such teaching makes evangelism and missionary work futile. It permits rebels to rage unchecked, uncorrected and unconverted.

Seeds grow.

Good Seed or bad Seed.

Right Seeds or wrong Seeds. Truth or error.

Anything that is sown into the soil of a human mind will grow. The mind does not referee what is right or wrong. It merely grows *any* Seed received into its soil.

It happened. The bad Seed came up. The soul winning pastor eventually resigned his church. He began a little prayer group. I watched as his influence in the community waned and died. It still stuns me today as I write this to you.

When Satan Wants To Destroy You, He Brings Someone Into Your Life. The Apostle Paul cautioned, "That we henceforth be no more children, tossed to and fro, and carried about with every wind of doctrine, by the sleight of men, *and* cunning craftiness, whereby they lie in wait to deceive;" (Ephesians 4:14).

Test all teaching by the entire Word of God. "Beware lest any man spoil you through philosophy and vain deceit, after the tradition of men, after the rudiments of the world, and not after Christ" (Colossians 2:8).

The Test Of Truth Is By The Product It Produces.

Reject the doctrines of men. "Touch not; taste not; handle not; Which all are to perish with the using; after the commandments and doctrines of men?" (Colossians 2:21,22).

Beware The Spirit Of Domination

Avoid the manipulation of controlling leaders. Important discipleship training has often been tainted and distorted by controlling leaders and teachers. Paul warned. "Let no man therefore judge you in meat, or in drink, or in respect of an holy day, or of the new moon, or of the sabbath *days*: Which are a shadow of things to come; but the body *is* of Christ" (Colossians 2:16,17).

Let me explain. Some months ago, a young lady decided to attend my Sunday services. Her home church was several hundred miles away. She felt impressed of the Holy Spirit to come and receive more teaching on His companionship. It created a furor in her home church. She was called in by the leaders of her church and interrogated intensely. She was informed that she could not attend another church *unless her leaders had sat in services there first.*

They would not give her permission to attend. This may shock you, but it is happening in hundreds of churches across our nation today. *It is not the spiritual strength of these controlling leaders that grants that position, but the weaknesses of saints who ignorantly follow them.* "For there are many unruly and vain talkers and deceivers, specially they of the circumcision: Whose mouths must be stopped, who subvert whole houses, teaching things which they ought not, for filthy lucre's sake" (Titus 1:10,11).

Advisors *advise.*
Leaders *lead.*
Counselors *counsel.*
Controllers *control.*
Tyrants *terrorize.*
Be careful of those who desire to make your decisions for you. The True Mentor advises you but does not control you. The True Mentor does not keep you connected to him but teaches you how to develop an addiction to God Himself.

Beware Prejudiced Teaching Concerning The Holy Spirit

Prejudiced teaching against the Holy Spirit could prevent the completion of your Assignment. Jesus promised the disciples, "And I will pray the Father, and He shall give you another Comforter, that He may abide with you for ever; Even the Spirit of truth; Whom the world cannot receive, because it seeth Him not, neither knoweth Him: but ye know Him; for He dwelleth with you, and shall be in you," (John 14:16,17).

I am so thankful for my unforgettable and irreplaceable companionship of the Holy Spirit. I experienced a marvelous baptism at a very young age. But, He touched my life in a dramatic and unexplainable way on July 13, 1994. I will never be the same again. I would give up every discovery, any Wisdom and knowledge I have known from childhood (including the alphabet and my ability to even speak) for what I have known and experienced through the Holy Spirit on that Wednesday at 7:00 a.m. in my bedroom.

I urge you to *pursue* a daily and hourly relationship with the Holy Spirit.

Sing to Him.
Love Him.
Talk to Him.
Discuss every part of your life with Him.
Listen to Him.
Honor Him.
The Holy Spirit is to us today what Jesus was to the twelve

disciples. What Jesus is to an unbeliever, the Holy Spirit is to the believer.

The Holy Spirit is to your prayer life what Jesus is to your salvation. He *is* Life. "For in Him we live, and move, and have our being;" (Acts 17:28).

The Holy Spirit is the Source of love, joy, peace and even your faith itself. "Thou wilt shew me the path of life: in Thy presence is fulness of joy; at Thy right hand there are pleasures for evermore" (Psalm 16:11).

Jesus is your daily Intercessor in Heaven. "Wherefore He is able also to save them to the uttermost that come unto God by Him, seeing He ever liveth to make intercession for them" (Hebrews 7:25). "It is Christ that died, yea rather, that is risen again, Who is even at the right hand of God, Who also maketh intercession for us" (Romans 8:34).

The Holy Spirit makes intercession for you on earth. "Likewise the Spirit also helpeth our infirmities: for we know not what we should pray for as we ought: but the Spirit Himself maketh intercession for us with groanings which cannot be uttered. And He that searcheth the hearts knoweth what is the mind of the Spirit, because He maketh intercession for the saints according to the will of God" (Romans 8:26,27).

Any error regarding the Holy Spirit could sabotage the entire mentorship system of the Holy Spirit in your life. This could distort every experience and information entering your mind.

Beware Of False Teaching Concerning Sickness And Healing

Be alert to error regarding Divine healing. Thousands have been taught that sickness comes from God as a teacher. Of course, the Bible declares that the Holy Spirit will teach us. "But the Comforter, which *is* the Holy Ghost, Whom the Father will send in My name, He shall teach you all things, and bring all things to your remembrance, whatsoever I have said unto you" (John 14:26).

Jesus came to destroy the works of the devil.

Jesus healed the sick. "How God anointed Jesus of Nazareth with the Holy Ghost and with power: Who went about doing good, and healing all that were oppressed of the devil; for God was with Him" (Acts 10:38).

Jesus *never* saw sickness as a teacher.

He treated disease as an *enemy.*

He *destroyed* it.

When I first entered the ministry as a church evangelist, I was nineteen years old. I had a prayer line during a service in south Louisiana. I can still see the lady standing before me even now as I write.

"Do you believe God wants to heal you?" I asked.

"Well, I believe He wants to *teach* me something through this sickness," was her reply.

She kept refusing to embrace with great faith the fact that God *wanted* her healed. Finally, exasperated, I asked her, "Are you taking any medicine?"

"Yes, I am taking lots of medicine," she replied.

"Naughty, naughty, naughty!" I teased. "If God wants you to be sick, and He is teaching you through disease, then why are you sneaking behind His back trying to get well?"

If God wants you ill, every doctor, nurse and hospital is a monument of rebellion and defiance to His plan.

Beware False Teaching Regarding Poverty And Prosperity

Much error is being taught regarding financial blessing. Some teach that if you are truly serving the Lord with all of your heart, your wealth is guaranteed. Yet, thousands of the wealthy are complete rebels to the will of God. Jesus often warned the rich and those who desired to be wealthy. "Take heed, and beware of covetousness: for a man's life consisteth not in the abundance of the things which he possesseth" (Luke 12:15).

James warned, "Your riches are corrupted, and your garments are motheaten. Your gold and silver is cankered; and the rust of them shall be a witness against you, and shall eat your flesh as it were fire. Ye have heaped treasure together for the last days" (James 5:2,3).

Wealth is not necessarily the proof of obedience nor the approval of God.

Yet, in contradiction to this, some have swung the pendulum the other way.

Some feel guilty for pursuing financial blessing and abundance. Yet, financial promises are continuously made in Scripture to those who enter into a covenant of sowing and reaping with the Lord of the Harvest.

Provision is promised to the sower. "Give, and it shall be given unto you; good measure, pressed down, and shaken together, and running over, shall men give into your bosom. For with the same measure that ye mete withal it shall be measured to you again" (Luke 6:38).

Protection is promised to the tither. "Bring ye all the tithes into the storehouse, that there may be meat in Mine house, and prove Me now herewith, saith the Lord of hosts, if I will not open you the windows of heaven, and pour you out a blessing, that there shall not be room enough to receive it. And I will rebuke the devourer for your sakes, and he shall not destroy the fruits of your ground; neither shall your vine cast her fruit before the time in the field, saith the Lord of hosts" (Malachi 3:10,11).

Plenty is promised to givers. "Honour the Lord with thy substance, and with the firstfruits of all thine increase: So shall thy barns be filled with plenty, and thy presses shall burst out with new wine" (Proverbs 3:9,10).

Blessing is promised to the obedient. "And it shall come to pass, if thou shalt hearken diligently unto the voice of the Lord thy God, to observe and to do all His commandments which I command thee this day, that the Lord thy God will set thee on high above all nations of the earth: And all these blessings shall come on thee, and overtake thee, if thou shalt hearken unto the voice of the Lord thy God" (Deuteronomy 28:1,2).

"If God really wants me to have money, He will give it to me," was the sardonic observation of a cynic in a recent crusade.

"Yes, I understand your philosophy. If He wanted your hair combed, He would have combed it for you this morning," was my reply.

Another cynic said, "Dr. Mike, don't you believe the devil will give you a lot of money to make you backslide away from God?"

"Then, why has he not overdosed you with finances?" was

my reply. When satan wanted to destroy Job, he did not double his income. He stole it.

What satan steals, God returns double. Read Job 42 very carefully. Read it aloud. Read it often. "And the Lord turned the captivity of Job, when he prayed for his friends: also the Lord gave Job twice as much as he had before...So the Lord blessed the latter end of Job more than his beginning:" (Job 42:10,12).

God *blessed* him.

God *provided.*

God gave him *finances.*

God gave him *provision.*

Jesus described His difference from false prophets very clearly. "The thief cometh not, but for to steal, and to kill, and to destroy: I am come that they might have life, and that they might have it more abundantly" (John 10:10).

Your Heavenly Father is well aware of your financial needs. "Your heavenly Father knoweth that ye have need of all these things" (Matthew 6:32).

Jesus taught that spiritual priorities produce provision. "But seek ye first the kingdom of God, and His righteousness; and all these things shall be added unto you" (Matthew 6:33). The teaching of Jesus was twofold: First, the Provider. Second, the Provision.

Jesus taught that our Father was a Giver, the true Source of every good and perfect gift. "If ye then, being evil, know how to give good gifts unto your children, how much more shall your Father which is in heaven give good things to them that ask Him?" (Matthew 7:11).

Second, Jesus taught that obedience produces supernatural provision for you. "But seek ye first the kingdom of God, and His righteousness; and all these things shall be added unto you" (Matthew 6:33).

Oh, run from error! Refuse to even receive it into your spirit or mind. Never negotiate with falsehood.

One Seed In The Mind Can Destroy A Lifetime Of Blessing.

4 Keys In Discerning Error

1. *You Must Study The Word Of God For Yourself.* "Study to shew thyself approved unto God, a workman that needeth not

to be ashamed, rightly dividing the Word of truth" (2 Timothy 2:15). Studying truth births the recognition of error.

2. *Refuse Conversation With Those Who Are Obsessed With Questions Instead Of Solutions.* "But shun profane *and* vain babblings: for they will increase unto more ungodliness...But foolish and unlearned questions avoid, knowing that they do gender strifes. And the servant of the Lord must not strive; but be gentle unto all *men*, apt to teach, patient," (2 Timothy 2:16,23,24).

3. *Enter The Secret Place And Listen To The Holy Spirit, Your Mentor* (read John 14-16). One hour with the Holy Spirit will transform your discerning ability.

4. *Recognize That Truth Will Bring Joy And Great Liberty; Error Brings Bondage, Fear And Depression.* "And ye shall know the truth, and the truth shall make you free" (John 8:32).

4 Facts About The Spirit Of Error

▶ Error enters your life through a *person.*

▶ Error enters your life during a season of *great need.*

▶ Error enters your life to *distract* you.

▶ Error increases agitation, frustration and *fear.*

"For the vile person will speak villany, and his heart will work iniquity, to practice hypocrisy, and to utter error against the Lord, to make empty the soul of the hungry, and he will cause the drink of the thirsty to fail" (Isaiah 32:6).

The secret of the obedient life is not in understanding error, but in pursuing *truth.*

When I was young, I encountered great internal frustration in my pursuit of truth. I always had a fear of believing a lie. I was quite concerned that perhaps I was influenced too greatly by my parents. I reasoned, "What if Daddy is wrong? What if Mother is merely repeating the teachings she has heard from her childhood? How do I *really* know if I am following the *truth*?"

So I began to gather various books on different cults, religions and belief systems. I wanted to study them for myself. I was defiant, rebellious and insistent that *everybody* had a view worth considering.

While in prayer, the Holy Spirit revealed a powerful truth to me: *It is impossible to understand error.* You have to be perverted to accept the perversion. My exhaustive study of cults, doctrines of men and belief systems would not bring me to a satisfying conclusion.

Jesus alone was Truth.

When Truth consumes you, error has no place within you. A friend told me that when bank tellers are being taught to distinguish counterfeit money, they are not given any phony money. Rather, they are given piles and piles of real money, *genuine* currency, to handle. When they have handled genuine currency repeatedly enough then something in the counterfeit is recognized *instantly.* They discern the false money because they have studied the genuine currency.

The Word of God is the true standard for discerning error. Absorb His Word and His presence so often that when something *contrary* to the Holy Spirit enters, *you will discern it instantly.* "Lest satan should get an advantage of us: for we are not ignorant of his devices" (2 Corinthians 2:11).

Our Prayer Together...

"Father, I pray for my special friend today who is reading Your revelation on his Assignment. I ask You to reveal truth in every part of his life. Reveal truth about Your healing presence, Your financial provision and about the Holy Spirit. Do not let us continue in any error. We hate falsehood and every evil way. We despise the doctrines of men but hunger for righteousness. *Purify our minds*, sanctify our hearts and provide a wall of protection around us that we would never fall into the pitfalls of prejudiced teaching, erroneous teaching and error. We have confidence that You will *protect* our minds and hearts, and will keep us focused on total obedience to Your plan for our lives. Make the Word come alive in us. Let Your words be like fire to purge and burn out anything unlike You. Help us to conquer and destroy the carnal and fleshly nature of our lives and permit the Holy Spirit to consume us. I ask this humbly and with all that is within me, in Jesus' name. Amen."

Remember: *Wrong Mentorship Can Paralyze Your Progress Toward Your Assignment.*

The Difference
Between Obscurity
And Significance
Is An Enemy.

-MIKE MURDOCK

∼ 30 ∼

WHEN YOU DISCOVER YOUR ASSIGNMENT, YOU WILL DISCOVER YOUR ENEMY.

You Will Always Have An Enemy.

When Joseph discovered his Assignment and shared it with his brothers, they quickly reacted. They sold him into slavery.

When Esther became queen, she soon discovered Haman. He was the enemy of her people, the Jews. He was conspiring to destroy them all.

When Nehemiah received permission from the king to rebuild the walls of Jerusalem, his enemies emerged. The warfare began.

When Jesus was born in Bethlehem, King Herod immediately took action to have Him killed.

When Jesus began His active ministry, the Pharisees opposed Him at every turn and eventually agreed with His crucifixion.

Discovering your Assignment is wonderful, energizing and thrilling. Watching the Miracle Hand of God connect you with strategic relationships is so stimulating and exciting.

But, you have an enemy.

You will *always* have an enemy.

Your enemy has recognized your Assignment.

9 Facts You Should Know About Your Assignment And Your Enemy

The Goal Of Your Enemy Is Broken Focus.

1. *Do Not Permit Your Focus To Be Shifted To Your Enemy.*

"Mike, I was so excited about my new church," the words gushed out of a young preacher's mouth late one night as we talked in his living room. "I felt like this was Heaven on earth. The people loved me. My family loved the new city. Everything was perfect. Then, suddenly out of nowhere one of the men of the church spread a false accusation against me. It has devastated me. I do not know which way to turn. What should I do? Did I *miss* the will of *God*?"

"Actually, this probably *confirms* that you are in the center of the will of God," I replied.

His enemy had *reacted*.

2. *Every Move In The Right Direction Will Be Confronted By Your Enemy.* Demons are assigned geographically just like angels and humans. When satan discovers that you are pursuing the center of your Assignment, demons will be assigned to prevent your entry into the next season, break your focus and *dilute your joy.*

3. *Recognize The Value Of An Enemy.* Your enemy is a *signpost* permitted by God to *confirm* that you are truly *entering* the greatest season of your life.

4. *Your Enemy Causes Movement.* The Israelites would have remained in Egypt had their afflictions not become unbearable.

5. *Your Enemy Reveals The Necessity Of God.* Without a conflict, we often become arrogant, self-centered and self-sufficient.

6. *Your Enemy Is The Only Obstacle Between Obscurity And Greatness.* David, without a Goliath, was just another shepherd boy. After he killed Goliath, he was known to all Israel.

7. *Your Assignment Forces Your Enemy To Reveal Himself.* As Jesus obeyed the Father, preaching and healing the sick, His enemies could not stifle their reaction and hatred.

8. *Your Enemy Forces Your Future To Become Visible.* Goliath positioned David for visibility. His future as a military champion became established.

9. *Your Enemy Is An Announcement That The Future You Have Longed For Has Arrived.* Goliath provided David an opportunity to demonstrate his difference from others.

Remember: *When You Discover Your Assignment, You Will Discover Your Enemy.*

❦ 31 ❦

YOUR RISE TO LEADERSHIP WILL REQUIRE EXCELLENCE IN YOUR PRESENT ASSIGNMENT.

Leadership Is Earned.

Before Ruth became the wife of wealthy Boaz, she *served* as a handmaiden to Naomi, her mother-in-law (read Ruth 1-4).

Before Joseph became second in command of Egypt, he *served* Potiphar and the prison system (see Genesis 39-41).

Before David became king of Israel, he *served* King Saul (see 1 Samuel 16:14-23).

Jesus taught that serving well decides your rise to greatness. "But whosoever will be great among you, let him be your minister; And whosoever will be chief among you, let him be your servant:" (Matthew 20:26,27). Jesus instructed His disciples that whoever wanted to be greatest among them must *first* become their servant. Sometimes you want to prosper first, then serve. But Jesus taught that servanthood preceded promotion.

Leadership is earned through servanthood.

Arrogance can cost you your Assignment. When King Saul ceased to have the heart of a servant, he ceased to prosper.

Uncommon Leaders have simply recognized the value of others. Humility is not thinking you are worthless. It is recognition of the worth and value of *others*. It is the willingness to help someone else succeed even if it requires that you step aside.

Your willingness to suffer qualifies you for eventual rulership. "If we suffer, we shall also reign with *Him*: if we deny *Him* He also will deny us:" (2 Timothy 2:12).

4 Important Facts About Excellence In Serving

"Humble yourselves therefore under the mighty hand of God,

that He may exalt you in due time:" (1 Peter 5:6).
   ▶ Servanthood is *instructed* by God.
   ▶ Servanthood is *expected* by God.
   ▶ Servanthood will always be *rewarded* at the appropriate
      time.
   ▶ Servanthood eventually becomes *rulership.*
   Remember: *Your Rise To Leadership Will Require Excellence
In Your Present Assignment.*

Our Prayer Together...

"Father, use these Seeds of Wisdom on Assignment to grow an Uncommon Harvest of peace, productivity and supernatural love for others. Use us to heal, restore, strengthen and bring many into a life of total obedience to You. We give ourselves to You and the Assignment You have commanded. In Jesus' name. Amen."

THE WISDOM LIBRARY OF MIKE MURDOCK

VOLUME 2

THE ASSIGNMENT:
THE PAIN &
THE PASSION

You Are Genetically Perfect
For The Environment
To Which God Has Assigned You.

-MIKE MURDOCK

❧ 32 ❧

THE PROBLEM GOD CREATED YOU TO SOLVE ON EARTH IS YOUR ASSIGNMENT.

⟾▸◦◂⟾

You Are Here For A Reason.

To assign means to set apart or mark for a specific purpose. "But know that the Lord hath set apart him that is godly for Himself:" (Psalm 4:3).

The Bible, The Manufacturer's Handbook, is filled with examples of those who discovered and embraced their Assignment.

▶ *Moses* solved problems for the *Israelites*.
▶ *Aaron* solved problems for *Moses*.
▶ *Jonathan* was assigned to *David*.
▶ *Jonah* was assigned to the *Ninevites*.
▶ A *handmaiden* helped *Naaman* get healed.
▶ *Ruth* was assigned to *Naomi*.

You, too, are assigned to solve problems.

For somebody.

Somewhere.

You are the *Healer* for someone sick.

You are the *Life jacket* for someone drowning.

You are the *Ruler* over someone unruly.

You are the *Lifter* for someone fallen.

You have asked these questions a thousand times. *Why* am I here? Why *me*? What is my *purpose*? Is there *really* a God? Where did I come from? Did I exist in another world before this one?

A poem is the proof of a *poet*.

A song is the proof of a *composer*.

A product is the proof of a *manufacturer*.

Creation is the proof of the *Creator*.

Why were you born? It is an excellent question. It is a wonderful question. It is a frequent question. It is an *answerable* question. You deserve an answer. The answers exist. The answers are clear. The answers are more obvious than many realize.

The Manufacturer is God.

The Product is You.

The Manual is the Bible.

▶ *You were created to bring pleasure to God (*see Revelation 4:11).

▶ *You have been set apart for an exclusive purpose and reason.* "But know that the Lord hath set apart him that is godly for Himself:" (Psalm 4:3).

▶ *You will give an account of your conduct and productivity.* "So then every one of us shall give account of himself to God" (Romans 14:12).

Every product contains more answers than we first realized. Study the car. The fact that it *moves* is proof that it has a different *purpose* than your home. Compare a baseball bat and a sandwich. The hardness of one and the softness of the other is an obvious *clue* that the purpose *differs.*

Studying your difference rather than your similarity to others will produce an incredible revelation of Wisdom. Especially regarding your Assignment—the problem you were created to solve.

Mechanics solve car problems.

Lawyers solve legal problems.

Ministers solve spiritual problems.

I had an interesting experience during a recent telephone conversation. While talking to someone very important in my life, I realized suddenly that I was merely listening. In fact, they asked me nothing. He did not ask me for my opinion, or feelings or observations. I waited patiently. Then, I thought, "Why am I even listening to this when he obviously does not want solutions or he would ask me questions?" Then it dawned on me. My *listening* was his solution. He simply needed someone to listen to his pain, discomfort and heartache. Yes, even listening to someone hurting near you is often a marvelous therapy and solution to their problem.

Motivational speakers receive thousands of dollars to solve

a problem for salesmen in a company. Effective counselors make an excellent living simply by being willing to listen patiently, thoughtfully, and consistently to their clients.

Sometimes, *words* heal.

Sometimes, *silence* heals.

Sometimes, *listening* heals.

It is important that you recognize your Assignment. It is essential that you embrace the *difference* in your Assignment. It is important that you are willing to be *mentored* for it.

Your function is *different* from others.

The *function* of others is different from yours.

Counselors provide *answers* to problems.

Comedians provide *escape* from problems.

Your Assignment is always to someone with a problem. Do not run from it. Embrace it.

9 Exciting Benefits Of Problems

1. Problems Are The Gates To Your Significance.
2. Problems Are Wonderful, Glorious Seeds For Change.
3. Problems Link You To Others.
4. Problems Provide Your Income.
5. Problems Birth Opportunity To Reveal Your Uniqueness.
6. Problems Birth New Relationships.
7. Problems Are The Real Reason Friendships Exist.
8. Remove Problems From The Earth, And You Will Destroy Any Sense Of Significance In Humanity.
9. Problems Bring Good People Together During Bad Times.

The mechanic knows that an automobile problem is his connection to you.

The lawyer knows that a legal problem is his connection to you.

The dentist knows that a tooth problem is his connection to you.

Remember: *The Problem God Created You To Solve On Earth Is Called Your Assignment.*

You Will Never Leave
Where You Are
Until You Decide Where
You Would Rather Be.

-MIKE MURDOCK

⇚ 33 ⇛

MOST PEOPLE NEVER DISCOVER THEIR OWN ASSIGNMENT.

No One Can Discover Your Assignment For You.

I read recently that the United States Department of Labor statistics revealed 70 percent of the work force of America is on the wrong job. Thousands *hate* their job. They despise getting up in the morning. They want more days off. They crave vacation time. They are unproductive, unhappy and dissatisfied with their work. Why? They simply have not discovered their own Assignment.

God intended for you to love your work. "...to rejoice in his labour; this is the gift of God" (Ecclesiastes 5:19).

Ask yourself the *right* questions.

Answer them *honestly*. Do you drag to your job every morning? Do you delay punching in your time clock as long as possible so you can have a few extra minutes of "freedom?" Do you stretch out your lunch and coffee breaks as far as you can? Do you rush out of the building at closing time? Do you sit by the punch-out clock fifteen minutes early, anxious to get home?

If so, it is obvious that you may be working on the wrong job. This is stealing time and money from your employer. This creates *guilt*.

Guilt always makes you critical of those in authority over you. This could explain why your life is not happy, productive or financially prosperous.

Many people never discover their own Assignment.

6 Reasons Many People Never Discover Their Own Assignment

1. *Many Do Not Even Know They Have An Assignment.*

Ignorance is devastating. Millions are not exposed to hearing the Word of God daily. Millions never attend the house of God where a man of God can *unlock* their destiny.

Your destiny is often unlocked in the presence of a man of God (read 1 Samuel 9 and 10). Saul knew little about his Assignment until he came into the presence of Samuel, the prophet. When he and his servant could not locate the donkeys for his father, the servant brought an *offering* to the man of God.

▶ That *Seed* was the Golden Connection to the *prophet*.

▶ The *prophet* was his Golden Link to his *destiny*.

2. *Many People Are Simply Impatient.* If it does not happen quickly, they quit. They refuse to invest the Seed of *Time*.

Uncommon men have uncommon patience. A fascinating story is told in 1 Kings 18:41-45. The prophet Elijah promised King Ahab that rain was about to fall. He went up to the top of Mount Carmel, "and he cast himself down upon the earth, and put his face between his knees, And said to his servant, Go up now, look toward the sea. And he went up, and looked, and said, There is nothing. And he said, Go again seven times. And it came to pass at the seventh time, that he said, Behold, there ariseth a little cloud out of the sea, like a man's hand. And he said, Go up, say unto Ahab, Prepare thy chariot, and get thee down, that the rain stop thee not. And it came to pass in the mean while, that the Heaven was black with clouds and wind, and there was a great rain" (1 Kings 18:42-45).

Elijah was powerful. What really made him powerful? Tenacity. Persistence. Determination. Unwillingness to quit. That is why he instructed his servant to look seven times. It appears that he even prayed again, and again and again. "Elias was a man subject to like passions as we are, and he prayed earnestly that it might not rain: and it rained not on the earth by the space of three years and six months. And he prayed again, and the Heaven gave rain, and the earth brought forth her fruit" (James 5:17,18).

3. *Many Succumb To Cultural Expectations Or Limited Community Opportunities.* Let me explain. Sometimes, your culture will expect women to do "women's" jobs. Men are expected to do "men's" jobs. Cultural expectations affect us. Moses was expected to continue being the general of the Egyptian army because he was the son of Pharaoh. He was raised in that culture.

God had a different plan.

Though it was painful, he withdrew from his culture and upbringing, and followed his Assignment in order to ensure long-term gain. "By faith Moses, when he was born, was hid three months of his parents, because they saw he was a proper child; and they were not afraid of the king's commandment. By faith Moses, when he was come to years, refused to be called the son of Pharaoh's daughter; Choosing rather to suffer affliction with the people of God, than to enjoy the pleasures of sin for a season; Esteeming the reproach of Christ greater riches than the treasures in Egypt: for he had respect unto the recompense of the reward. By faith he forsook Egypt, not fearing the wrath of the king: for he endured, as seeing Him Who is invisible. Through faith he kept the passover, and the sprinkling of blood, lest he that destroyed the firstborn should touch them" (Hebrews 11:23-28).

It is important to overcome the limitations of community opportunities. I have had conversations with people who explained their dilemma with their Assignment. "You just do not understand, Dr. Murdock!"

Champions *create* their own opportunities.

4. *Thousands Are Unwilling To Make Any Changes Or Leave Their Place Of Comfort In Order To Complete Their Assignment.*

The Scriptures are filled with illustrations of people who *moved* toward their geographical Assignment. Ruth left Moab and experienced her relationship with Boaz in Bethlehem. Abraham left his kinfolks. "By faith Abraham, when he was called to go out into a place which he should after receive for an inheritance, obeyed; and he went out, not knowing whither he went" (Hebrews 11:8).

5. *Most People Are Unwilling To Fight For Their Assignment.* Obedience requires warfare. Battle is normal in the life of an achiever. Thousands want to avoid confrontation with people, family and, especially, demonic spirits.

Your Assignment will always require confrontation with someone. You have an enemy.

David had Goliath.

Daniel had lions.

Esther had Haman.

Champions do warfare. "Who through faith subdued kingdoms, wrought righteousness, obtained promises, stopped the mouths of lions, Quenched the violence of fire, escaped the edge of the sword, out of weakness were made strong, waxed valiant in fight, turned to flight the armies of the aliens. Women received their dead raised to life again: and others were tortured, not accepting deliverance; that they might obtain a better resurrection: And others had trial of *cruel* mockings and scourgings, yea, moreover of bonds and imprisonment: They were stoned, they were sawn asunder, were tempted, were slain with the sword: they wandered about in sheepskins and goatskins; being destitute, afflicted, tormented; (Of Whom the world was not worthy:) they wandered in deserts, and in mountains, and in dens and caves of the earth" (Hebrews 11:33-38).

You will never be happy or satisfied until you are in the *center* of your expertise, your Assignment. This explains the incredible stories of people who left jobs worth millions for low salaries...to do exactly what they *loved*.

I read a few days ago of an attorney making $1,000,000 a year. He took a job at $30,000 a year, because it was relaxing. He now works with plants, which is what he loved all of his life. (If your hobby is more enjoyable than your work, your work should be related to your hobby.)

Fight for your Assignment. Go for it. You only have one life to live. Make your Assignment the center of your life.

6. *Many Become Obsessed With Their Weaknesses Instead Of Their Assignment.* God rebuked this in Jeremiah. "Then the word of the Lord came unto me, saying, Before I formed thee in the belly I knew thee; and before thou camest forth out of the womb I sanctified thee, and I ordained thee a prophet unto the nations. Then said I, Ah, Lord God! behold, I cannot speak: for I am a child. But the Lord said unto me, Say not, I am a child: for thou shalt go to all that I shall send thee, and whatsoever I command thee thou shalt speak" (Jeremiah 1:4-7). Jeremiah felt like a child. God instructed him not to discuss his weakness. His *Assignment* was to be his focus.

3 Important Facts About Your Weaknesses

1. *Uncommon Men Are Always Aware Of Their*

Weaknesses. Moses was obsessed with his inability to speak. So, God *staffed* his weakness by providing *Aaron.* God wanted his focus to be on his Assignment to the Israelites.

David felt uncomfortable in the armor of Saul. So, God provided an appropriate weapon, the slingshot.

The widow of Zarephath was overwhelmed by the effects of the famine. Elijah had to remind her that the last meal she presently possessed was the Seed that would produce what she needed.

2. *Your Weakness Is An Ideal Place For God To Reveal His Supernatural Power.* "But God hath chosen the foolish things of the world to confound the wise; and God hath chosen the weak things of the world to confound the things which are mighty; And base things of the world, and things which are despised, hath God chosen, yea, and things which are not, to bring to nought things that are: That no flesh should glory in His presence. But of Him are ye in Christ Jesus, Who of God is made unto us wisdom, and righteousness, and sanctification, and redemption:" (1 Corinthians 1:27-30).

3. *The Presence And Power Of God Is Always More Than Enough To Overcome Your Weakness.* "Be not afraid of their faces: for I am with thee to deliver thee, saith the Lord. Then the Lord put forth His hand, and touched my mouth. And the Lord said unto me, Behold, I have put My words in thy mouth. See, I have this day set thee over the nations and over the kingdoms, to root out, and to pull down, and to destroy, and to throw down, to build, and to plant" (Jeremiah 1:8-10).

Remember: *Most People Never Discover Their Own Assignment.*

When Jesus Wanted To Create
A Great Miracle -
He Always Gave
A Small Instruction.

-MIKE MURDOCK

☙ 34 ☙

YOUR ASSIGNMENT MAY HAVE SMALL BEGINNINGS.

Little Things Matter.

Small hinges control huge doors. Small keys unlock vaults containing millions of dollars. A little steering determines the direction of a huge semi-truck. One small finger dialing the telephone can start a business transaction of one billion dollars. *Never despise small beginnings.* "For who hath despised the day of small things?" (Zechariah 4:10).

Many will never achieve a great Assignment because they want their beginning to be spectacular. I am reminded of the fascinating story of Naaman, the captain of the host of the king of Syria. He was a leper. When he went to the house of Elisha, the prophet sent him a simple instruction. Elisha sent a message to him to go and wash in the Jordan River seven times. Naaman was infuriated. He had a different mental picture of how his healing would occur. One of his servants made an interesting statement, "My father, if the prophet had bid thee do some great thing, wouldest thou not have done it? how much rather then, when he saith to thee, Wash, and be clean?" (2 Kings 5:13).

The Assignment from Elisha was simple, clear and direct. Naaman was to go wash in Jordan seven times.

When You Do The Simple, The Supernatural Occurs.

Small Beginnings Often Have Great Endings.

Jesus understood this principle. He was born in a stable. His beginning was in a small town of Bethlehem. It did not matter to Him, because He knew His destiny. He was aware of the greatness of His *destination.* One of His greatest statements ever is, "He that is faithful in that which is least is faithful also in much: and he that is unjust in the least is unjust also in much" (Luke 16:10).

Attention To Details Produces Excellence. It is the difference between extraordinary champions and losers. So, do not despise and feel insignificant in your small acts of obedience while giving birth to your Assignment.

One of the great evangelists of our day began his ministry duplicating tapes for his mentor. Hour after hour, day after day, he sat and duplicated tapes. He listened to each tape over and over. He served. He ministered. He assisted. It was the *beginning* of a significant ministry.

Ruth began as an ignorant Moabite heathen girl. Her attention to the small details of her Assignment, Naomi, positioned her as the great-grandmother of David and ushered in the lineage of Jesus.

Abigail brought lunch to the starving man, David. She became his wife.

When Jesus Wanted To Produce A Great Miracle, He Always Gave A Small Instruction.

Little things mattered to Him. Notice the small, insignificant instructions that Jesus gave. They almost seemed ridiculous. Some might think these were instructions given to children, but none of them were. Rather, they were given to grown men, to mature adults.

"Go, wash in the pool of Siloam," (John 9:7). A big miracle? Yes, a blind man was healed from a lifetime of blindness.

"Launch out into the deep, and let down your nets for a draught" (Luke 5:4). This small instruction produced the *greatest catch of fish the disciples had ever gathered.*

"Fill the waterpots with water" (John 2:7). It produced the *greatest wine* anyone had tasted, ever. It happened at the marriage of Canaan.

"Arise, and take up thy bed, and go thy way into thine house" (Mark 2:11). What was the result? A man sick of the palsy, *immediately arose*, took up his bed, and went forth before them all and many glorified God because of it.

"Bring them hither to Me" (Matthew 14:18). These words were spoken regarding the five loaves and two fishes, the lunch of a lad. What happened afterwards has been preached around the world. *Thousands were fed miraculously*, and at the conclusion, each of the twelve disciples had a basketful to bring home!

▶ Great miracles do not require great instructions.

▶ Great miracles require *obeyed* instructions.

A student in Bible school sits in chapel daily awaiting a neon sign in the heavens declaring, "Bob, go to Calcutta, India." It never happens. Why? Bob has not obeyed the *first* instruction. "Bob, go to the prayer room at 7:00 a.m."

Obedience Turns A Common Instruction Into An Uncommon Miracle.

God does not give great instructions to great men.

God Gives Uncommon Instructions To Common Men. But when you *obey* that instruction, *greatness* is birthed. "If ye be willing and obedient, ye shall eat the good of the land:" (Isaiah 1:19).

Nothing you will do today is small in the eyes of God.

Remember: *Your Assignment May Have Small Beginnings.*

You Cannot Be
What You Are Not,
But You Can Become
What You Are Not.

-MIKE MURDOCK

❧ 35 ❧

YOUR ASSIGNMENT WAS SCHEDULED BEFORE YOUR BIRTH.

God Plans Ahead.

You were destined for this very time in history. Throughout the precious Scriptures, we see many illustrations of how God is involved with the unborn before a mother ever sees the face of her child.

God scheduled the birth of *Samson.* It is written, "for I have been a Nazarite unto God from my mother's womb:" (Judges 16:17).

God scheduled the birth of *David.* "But thou art He that took me out of the womb: Thou didst make me hope when I was upon my mother's breasts. I was cast upon Thee from the womb: Thou art my God from my mother's belly" (Psalm 22:9,10).

God scheduled the birth of *Isaiah.* Isaiah acknowledged that it was "...the Lord that formed me from the womb to be His servant," (Isaiah 49:5).

God scheduled the birth of *John the Baptist,* "For he shall be great in the sight of the Lord, and shall drink neither wine nor strong drink; and he shall be filled with the Holy Ghost, even from his mother's womb. And many of the children of Israel shall he turn to the Lord their God" (Luke 1:15).

God scheduled the birth of *Jesus.* Jesus prayed, "Father, I will that they also, whom Thou hast given Me, be with Me where I am; that they may behold My glory, which Thou hast given Me: for Thou lovedst Me before the foundation of the world. O righteous Father, the world hath not known Thee: but I have known Thee, and these have known that Thou hast sent Me" (John 17:24,25).

God scheduled the birth of the *Apostle Paul.* "But when it

pleased God, Who separated me from my mother's womb, and called me by His grace," (Galatians 1:15).

God has scheduled *your birth*. "According as He hath chosen us in Him before the foundation of the world, that we should be holy and without blame before Him in love:" (Ephesians 1:4).

Yes, it is true. Samson, David, Isaiah, John the Baptist, Jesus and Paul all were chosen and called by God before their birth. Then, Paul tells you and me that God chose us prior to our birth, *even before the world was created*. This is wonderful! This is a glorious fact that you should embrace at this point in your life!

God created this *earth*.

God created *you*.

God *wanted* you *here*.

This is proof you were made *for a purpose*.

You have a *Divine* and *decided* Assignment to fulfill on the earth.

You have every right to be here.

Remember: *Your Assignment Was Scheduled Before Your Birth*.

~ 36 ~

YOUR ASSIGNMENT WILL TAKE YOU WHERE YOU HAVE NEVER BEEN BEFORE.

━━━━━◆◉◆━━━━━

Changes Are Often Uncomfortable.
When God gives you an Assignment, those seasons of discomfort are merely *bridges* to the greatest visitations of your lifetime—even if you have never been there before.

Moses went where he had never been before. Moses was sent to be the deliverer of the children of Israel. Then, God took them where none of them had *ever* gone before.

Joseph went where he had never been before. Joseph was sold by his brothers to a caravan of Ishmaelites. They sold him into Egypt, a new location and new country for him. Yet, it was there that he became second in command of the entire country.

Ruth went where she had never been before. Ruth left her native land of Moab to serve her mother-in-law, Naomi. Yes, it was a strange place and a strange lifestyle, but it was there that Ruth found the golden link to the man of her lifetime, Boaz.

Sometimes those around you are unqualified to celebrate your uniqueness. So, God takes you to *another place* where your value will be embraced and pursued.

None of these champions knew *how* God was going to direct their lives. They simply knew God. They *trusted* Him. The *will of God* mattered, as much as the *place* where He led them mattered.

Embrace this truth. *Your Assignment may take you places you never thought you would see.* Uncomfortable places. Unique places. Difficult places. I love comfort. In fact, I do not like leaving the United States at all. For several years now, I have turned down many speaking invitations I have received from all over the world because I love the comfort of predictable climates and circumstances.

A Season Of Discomfort Often Produces Rewards For A Lifetime

Many years ago, one of my dear friends, a great missionary in East Africa, wrote me a letter. "Mike, please pray about going with me to Nairobi, Kenya. We are opening up a great Christian Center. I want you to hold the first major crusade with me there."

I cannot describe for you the immense discomfort I had my first days in East Africa. I did not like the taste of the food. I did not like driving on the "wrong" side of the highway! It was almost impossible for me to use any of my American illustrations in my messages because the people would not have understood anything I said. I had to speak *slowly* so the interpreter could understand me. Occasionally, he misinterpreted my message entirely and the people did not get the message that I was delivering.

Yet, today some of the greatest memories of my life are linked to five outstanding trips to East Africa. Almost one year of my life was spent in that great country preaching the glorious gospel of Jesus Christ. In fact, a number of children over there were named after me because I was responsible for the spiritual birth of their parents.

The Poland Report

Many years ago, I completed a crusade in Brazil and flew on to East Africa for another crusade. Concluding the crusades in East Africa, I drove all night and day in a small, cramped taxi from the interior of Tanzania to the coast. It took 14 hours. It was one of the most difficult trips of my life as I made my way into the airport, where I waited many more hours for the plane to leave for Germany. When I arrived in Germany, I had to wait more hours to fly to Poland. When I arrived in Poland, I had a six-hour ride in the back of another small taxi with all of my luggage piled high around me.

When I finally got there, after three days of flying, buried under my luggage, I preached for three hours. When I finished, the people begged me to keep going. They did not want to close the service. The secret police even came to visit the crusade and brought their families. My crusade was even held in the headquarters building of the communist party! I later learned from missionaries that the entire underground church in Poland doubled in those days of services. Here is a report I received recently from the missionary from those crusade services years ago.

"Mike, last week I returned from northern Poland, where I was invited to minister the Word of God in a church located in Lebork. The pastor of a growing church in that city, named Robert—though he was not a pastor yet when attending your meetings—and some of the people in the surrounding area were with us in Warsaw for your four-day seminar in November 1987. They gave me good reports and asked when you were coming to Poland again. Here are a couple of them:

One brother, named Kasik, who is a fisherman by occupation, told me that when you asked the people in the meeting hall to hold up their wallets believing for God's financial blessing, he held his up in faith, even though he was in debt and constantly borrowing money. *Today, he owes no man anything. He, his wife and their five children have their own home and car!*

When Robert, the pastor, attended your seminar, he lived in a small apartment, which he shared with his brother-in-law's family. He told me that your seminar inspired him to dream of building his own home and having a car. Today he and his wife have four children. *He has a car, and I stayed in one of the rooms of the home that he built. God's Word works."*

His letter continued, "In Warsaw, you may remember, brother Andrzej, who gave to the Lord the best that he had then when picking you up from Warsaw with his old green Fiat. Since then, he has owned several vehicles, among them was a Ford Scorpio. *Now his wife drives a Volkswagen Polo, and he has a BMW. He also owns his own large apartment.* He and his wife and three children are faithfully serving the Lord! Hallelujah!

Do you have any plans for returning to Poland?

In Christ Jesus,

Frank J. Olszewski"

I will never forget Poland. When I walked out of the crusade that night, the Holy Spirit spoke to me and said, "There is a *place* for you, a *purpose* for you and a *people* for you." I have never experienced anything like it in my lifetime. The spiritual hunger of the Polish people is indescribable. Perhaps, they have been oppressed so long that they soak up everything they hear like a sponge. It was tremendous. I never dreamed that I would go there and share the gospel with so many hungry souls. I thank God every week for my memories of Poland.

▶ *You have not yet been everywhere God is going to take you.*

▶ You may not have even been to the place where you are going to spend the rest of your life.

▶ Be ready for *changes. Dramatic* changes. *Bold* changes. *Radical* changes. *Unexpected* changes. *Miracle* changes. *Healing* changes. *Promotional* changes.

▶ Your *greatest* friends may still be in your *future.*

▶ God is connecting you with *new people, new truth* and *new provision.*

▶ You will not stay where you are.

Today is a temporary station where He has you changing planes.

Remember: *Your Assignment Will Take You Where You Have Never Been Before.*

❧ 37 ❧

YOUR ASSIGNMENT MAY BE TO BIRTH SOMETHING THAT HAS NEVER EXISTED BEFORE.

<hr/>

You Were Created To Change Somebody.

For a long time, the Jewish people had worshipped God in tents. When Solomon chose to build the Temple of the Lord, it was something that had never existed before in Israel. It was profound and awesome. Without a doubt it required uncommon faith and administrative capabilities.

Your Assignment may be so different, so extraordinary, that *no person has ever attempted it before.* If this happens, you may be tempted to become discouraged because you do not have a *pattern* before you.

Having an example is comforting. Having a role model of a champion who has done something before us can be a great motivation and encouragement.

However, God may be doing a different thing with your life— so different that He has not even entrusted your Assignment to another. *This is your season for birthing that Assignment.*

3 Essential Keys When You Receive A New Assignment

1. *Do Not Feel Obligated To Open Up Your Secret Longings To Everyone Near You.* Your closest friends and even your family may find it impossible to encourage you in this "new adventure." Stay quiet before the Lord. Do what Mary did. Simply ponder these things in your heart.

Somebody told me that if the eggs containing little chickens are broken too quickly, the little chicks will die. So, it is with the timing of your dreams and goals. Your Assignment contains seasons. Timing is crucial. Spend time in the presence of the Holy Spirit. Permit God to give you the exact plan for your Assignment.

2. *Discern The Difference Between The Command And The Plan.*

You see, the *command* is different from the *plan*. It took a moment for Noah to get the command. But it took many years to get the plan for building the ark. It was the *first* time an ark had ever been built.

3. *Restoration Is As Necessary As Creation.*

Your Assignment may be restoration and repair. Like Nehemiah, you may be called to rebuild something that has been broken down. It may require great Seeds of patience and investment of time. Negotiation may become a major tool. You may find it disheartening that people will not rally behind you and respond to your vision.

Do not become discouraged. Your Assignment was decided by God and was discovered by you. You do not have to prove it to anyone or force other people to grasp its value. Your obedience in following His instructions will bring you great joy.

Remember: *Your Assignment May Be To Birth Something That Has Never Existed Before.*

❧ 38 ❧

YOUR ASSIGNMENT MAY APPEAR RIDICULOUS, ILLOGICAL OR EVEN IMPOSSIBLE TO OTHERS.

God Never Uses Logic To Produce Miracles.

When the shepherd boy, David, faced Goliath, it appeared ridiculous. His slingshot looked like a toothpick next to the huge spear of the giant. His adolescent voice and naive countenance probably caused great laughter among the soldiers.

Even though he had killed a lion and a bear, I imagine David may have felt very uncomfortable. However, God had brought him there for a reason. He may have looked ridiculous and illogical, *but God was with him. It was The Assignment* (read 1 Samuel 17:1-51).

The only fact that matters is that God is with you.

It seemed impossible when Nehemiah set out to rebuild the burned and broken down walls of Jerusalem. But, somehow in the depths of his heart, Nehemiah had a mandate from God. It was not that he did not care. It was not a lack of sensitivity. Undoubtedly, he cried himself to sleep many nights in his bed feeling like the laughing stock of the entire country. *But, it was The Assignment* (see Nehemiah 2:12).

The crucifixion was torturous and impossible in the mind of Jesus. He must have felt that way when He cried out in the garden "let this cup pass from me." However, God works with long-range plans, not short-term popularity contests. *It was The Assignment* (see Matthew 26:39; 27:22-50).

It seemed ridiculous and illogical to walk around the walls of Jericho expecting them to fall. *But that was The Assignment* (see Joshua 6:3-5).

It was ridiculous for Naaman the leper to expect his healing by going into the Jordan River. *But, it was The Assignment* (see 2 Kings 5:10).

It was illogical for a blind man to expect a miracle by washing his face. Wiping clay and spittle off his face and walking two miles to wash it off must have brought a thousand conflicting thoughts through his mind. *But, it was The Assignment* (see John 9:6,7).

3 Facts You Should Understand About Illogical Instructions From God

1. *Instructions From God Are Often Illogical And Ridiculous To The Human Mind.* "Because the foolishness of God is wiser than men; and the weakness of God is stronger than men. But God hath chosen the foolish things of the world to confound the wise; and God hath chosen the weak things of the world to confound the things which are mighty; That no flesh should glory in His presence" (1 Corinthians 1:25,27,29).

2. *Illogical Instructions Are Given To Prevent Self-Sufficiency And Self-Worship.* "That no flesh should glory in His presence" (1 Corinthians 1:29).

3. *Uncommon Instructions Often Produce Uncommon Miracles.*

Do not despair when you receive an instruction in your prayer time that causes you to fear or dread carrying it out. Miracles are always on the other side of obedience. *Always.*

Remember, the seasons of your life will always change every time you decide to use your faith.

Remember: *Your Assignment May Appear Ridiculous, Illogical Or Even Impossible To Others.*

☞ 39 ☞

YOUR ASSIGNMENT MAY APPEAR AT FIRST TO BE A TOTAL CONTRADICTION TO YOUR GIFTS, SKILLS AND EXPERIENCE.

God Finds Genius Unnecessary.

The world worships the mind. Intellectualism is the god of the age. There is a giant whirlpool of words. Men create monuments of philosophy and concepts.

God laughs.

God can use you, gifted or not. "For it is written, I will destroy the wisdom of the wise, and will bring to nothing the understanding of the prudent. Where is the wise? where is the scribe? where is the disputer of this world? hath not God made foolish the wisdom of this world?" (1 Corinthians 1:19,20).

Sometimes God will give you an Assignment that appears to conflict with your gifts. You may lack the educational training. It may seem unnatural and uncomfortable for you.

He wants to *grow* you. So, He will choose someone like Gideon, Jephthah or a small shepherd boy to do something astounding. "But God hath chosen the foolish things of the world to confound the wise; and God hath chosen the weak things of the world to confound the things which are mighty;" (1 Corinthians 1:27).

It occurred in the life of David. He was accustomed to his little slingshot. He had been sitting with sheep on a hillside. His brothers were in battle. His father had sent him to bring food to them. As he approached the camp, he heard the shout of the huge giant, Goliath. David was not a professional soldier. He was untrained, untaught, and untried on the battlefield of war. King

Saul placed his armor around David. When David took the heavy and huge sword, he was distraught. You could almost see his face contort, "I am sorry, sir! I cannot use these weapons! I cannot wear this armor. It does not even fit me."

His Assignment appears to be a total contradiction to his experience. But, God finds the genius of battle unnecessary in this particular conflict. He simply needs *access* to a pure heart. The intellectualism of generals at a strategy table is a joke to God. "That no flesh should glory in his presence" (1 Corinthians 1:29).

Moses is another example. He complained to God that he could not talk well. He was incapable of conversing with Pharaoh. God used Aaron to be a voice for him. Yet, Moses became so skilled in communicating that he wrote songs and is considered the author of the first five books of the Bible under the inspiration of the Holy Spirit.

Some of the greatest preachers who have ever lived never even attended Bible college. They were totally dependent upon the Holy Spirit. Their hearts were pure before God.

What they lacked in *social* grace, they made up in the *saving* grace of the gospel.

What they lacked in *protocol,* they possessed in *power.*

Many great and effective healing ministers have never studied a course in Divine healing. They simply had faith in God. They were swift to *obey* God. Their academic achievements were minimal. There were no long degrees behind their name. They were not obsessed with using pompous words or asking rhetorical questions.

They simply hated sickness and disease.

They knew Jesus was the Healer.

Some of the greatest singers who have ever lived never had a singing lesson. But their hearts were full. Their God-given gift craved expression. Because of this, they touched millions of lives.

When God decides your Assignment, He does not examine your past to qualify you. He examines your *heart.* "Remember ye not the former things, neither consider the things of old. Behold, I will do a new thing; now it shall spring forth; shall ye not know it? I will even make a way in the wilderness, *and* rivers in the desert" (Isaiah 43:18,19).

Focus on the future you desire, not the failure you hate. Oh, my precious friend, please receive this instruction in the depths of your heart! Do not become fearful, uncertain and distraught at the presence of your enemy! Do not allow your weakness to become your focus. "Be not afraid of their faces: for I *am* with thee to deliver thee, saith the Lord" (Jeremiah 1:8).

Remember: *Your Assignment May Appear At First To Be A Total Contradiction To Your Gifts, Skills And Experience.*

A Miracle
Can Happen
As Quickly
As A Tragedy.

-MIKE MURDOCK

❧ 40 ❧

GOD CAN GET YOU ANYWHERE HE WANTS YOU WITHIN 24 HOURS.

━━━━━━❧❖❧━━━━━━

Miracles Happen As Quickly As Tragedies.

The financial status of Ruth changed within 24 hours. One day Ruth, the Moabite heathen girl, is standing in a barley field. She is a peasant woman. She is impoverished. Her husband is dead. Her father-in-law is dead. Her brother-in-law is dead. Her mother-in-law is so embittered that she has changed her own name.

Suddenly, she is Mrs. Boaz.

She lives in a big house with servants waiting on her hand and foot. In the modern-day scene, chauffeurs would be opening limousine doors for her.

God can get you anywhere He wants you...within 24 hours.

The personal prestige and influence of Joseph changed within 24 hours. Joseph is in prison. Perhaps, he is wearing striped clothes and eating out of a small metal plate. He has been falsely accused of raping the wife of a government leader.

Suddenly, within 24 hours, he is seated on a throne, wearing royal robes and overseeing the entire nation of Egypt. One day he is holding a broom in his hand; the next day, he is holding a scepter. He moves from poverty to wealth...within 24 hours. In fact, he gives each of his brothers a huge piece of real estate, a ranch of their own.

God can get you anywhere He wants you within 24 hours.

The confidence and authority of the disciples changed within 24 hours. The atmosphere is deadly. The sorrow has penetrated the homes. Jesus, the miracle worker, is gone. His body is laying in a tomb. The disciples are demoralized. Some even want to return to their fishing boats.

Suddenly, He has returned with a glorified body. He walks with them. He has a meal with them. It does not take long for incredible changes to begin. Your life can change dramatically within 24 hours.

As you obey the instructions of the Holy Spirit, you too will find miraculous turnarounds occurring. It will astonish you how quickly miracles can occur in your Assignment.

Remember: *God Can Get You Anywhere He Wants You Within 24 Hours.*

RECOMMENDED BOOKS
B-15   Seeds Of Wisdom On Miracles (32 pages/$3)

❧ 41 ❧

YOUR ASSIGNMENT MAY BE TO SOLVE AN EXISTING PROBLEM FOR SOMEONE WHOSE VERY SURVIVAL DEPENDS ON YOUR OBEDIENCE.

———————⟫➤•0•⟪⟨———————

You Are A Life Jacket To Somebody Close To You.

You are the *Master Key* to somebody in trouble. Esther discovered this. When the Jewish race was threatened with extinction, Mordecai said to Esther, "who knoweth whether thou art come to the kingdom for such a time as this?" (Esther 4:14). Mordecai had discovered a secret plot by a wicked man, Haman, one of the advisers to the king. There was going to be a complete annihilation of the Jews.

So, Mordecai sent a message to Esther. He insisted that she approach the king and expose Haman's evil intention. She was frightened because her life would be endangered. Protocol required the king to summon her. She was swift to fast and wait upon God.

God honored her. Favor came from the king. Haman was hung on the gallows and the Jews were permitted to protect themselves. Had Esther not obeyed her Assignment, thousands would have been slaughtered.

Somebody's future is always in your hands.

Joseph is a fascinating illustration. When his brothers sold him into slavery, he never became bitter. When they returned to Egypt for corn, he eventually told them who he was. He revealed that he was indeed their brother whom they had hated so long ago.

He discovered the key that released him from anxiety. He

saw *every* chapter of his life as an important *ingredient* in the plan of God. "And God sent me before you to preserve you a posterity in the earth, and to save your lives by a great deliverance" (Genesis 45:7). Had Joseph not carried out his Assignment, his own family and the entire Egyptian nation would have died from starvation.

Somebody needs something God has placed within you.

Warfare is distracting.

When you focus on the *obstacles* to your Assignment, you ignore the *significance* of your Assignment. It is so easy to get wrapped up in fighting your enemy, your Goliath, that you forget there's someone close to you whose future depends on your conquering.

Somebody is observing you today.

Somebody's entire future is in your hands this very moment.

Remember: *Your Assignment May Be To Solve An Existing Problem For Someone Whose Very Survival Depends On Your Obedience.*

∽ 42 ∽

YOUR ASSIGNMENT WILL BRING SOMEONE GREAT JOY.

Your Assignment Will End A Crisis For Someone.

The Assignment of Jonah brought joy to 120,000 people. Read carefully the book of Jonah. God was angry. The wickedness of Nineveh had come up before Him. So, God decided to assign Jonah to that city of 120,000 people. Jonah rebelled. God decided to educate him properly in the big fish. I call it, "Seaweed University." Jonah repented and "arose, and went unto Nineveh, according to the word of the Lord" (Jonah 3:3).

The people of Nineveh believed God. They proclaimed a fast, and put on sackcloth, "...from the greatest of them even to the least of them" (Jonah 3:5).

God responded favorably. "And God saw their works, that they turned from their evil way; and God repented of the evil, that He had said that He would do unto them; and He did it not" (Jonah 3:10).

An entire city experienced miraculous joy. The Assignment of one man brought joy to an entire city.

The Assignment of David caused thousands to dance with joy in the streets of his homeland. It happened after his Assignment against Goliath. The Philistines were routed by the Israelites. Joy filled the cities, and families began to dance and shout throughout the streets. "And it came to pass as they came, when David was returned from the slaughter of the Philistine, that the women came out of all cities of Israel, singing and dancing, to meet king Saul, with tabrets, with joy, and with instruments of musick. And the women answered one another as they played, and said, Saul hath slain his thousands, and David his ten thousands" (1 Samuel 18:6,7).

▶ When a man of God *obeys,* miracles flow.

▶ When miracles flow, joy *erupts.*

The Assignment of Elijah brought joy to the heart and home of an impoverished widow. Read 1 Kings 17 for an electrifying account of Elijah's encounter with the widow of Zarephath. "And the word of the Lord came unto him, saying, Arise, get thee to Zarephath, which belongeth to Zidon, and dwell there: behold, I have commanded a widow woman there to sustain thee. So he arose and went to Zarephath. And when he came to the gate of the city, behold, the widow woman was there gathering of sticks: and he called to her, and said, Fetch me, I pray thee, a little water in a vessel, that I may drink. And as she was going to fetch it, he called to her, and said, Bring me, I pray thee, a morsel of bread in thine hand. And she said, As the Lord thy God liveth, I have not a cake, but an handful of meal in a barrel, and a little oil in a cruse: and, behold, I am gathering two sticks, that I may go in and dress it for me and my son, that we may eat it, and die" (1 Kings 17:8-12).

The widow had one meal left between her and her son. He was dying. Can you imagine her emaciated body and tortured countenance? Her son was skin and bones. Life seemed almost over for them both. It seemed that her faith had not worked. Undoubtedly, she had sung songs of confidence in God. This day, she had no song.

You Are Never Closer To A Miracle Than When You Receive An Instruction From A Man Of God. "And Elijah said unto her, Fear not; go and do as thou hast said: but make me thereof a little cake first, and bring *it* unto me, and after make for thee and for thy son. For thus saith the Lord God of Israel, The barrel of meal shall not waste, neither shall the cruse of oil fail, until the day that the Lord sendeth rain upon the earth. And she went and did according to the saying of Elijah: and she, and he, and her house, did eat many days. And the barrel of meal wasted not, neither did the cruse of oil fail, according to the word of the Lord, which He spake by Elijah" (1 Kings 17:13-16).

Somewhere, a man of God received his Assignment from God. "Go to Zarephath."

His Assignment reversed the curse of hell against her life. His entry birthed a miracle.

His Assignment brought supernatural provision for the rest

of the famine.

The Assignment of Queen Esther brought an entire nation great joy. Haman was an enemy of all the Jews. He had conspired against the Jews to destroy them. But, Queen Esther came before the King. She exposed his wicked plans. The Jews were allowed to "gather themselves together, and to stand for their life, to destroy, to slay, and to cause to perish, all the power of the people and province that would assault them, both little ones and women, and to take the spoil of them for a prey," (Esther 8:11).

Joy filled the cities. "The Jews had light, and gladness, and joy, and honour" (Esther 8:16).

The Assignment of Joseph brought joy to a starving nation. Joseph became the prime minister of Egypt, second in power only to Pharaoh. Imagine the great joy he brought to his father and brothers when he provided them housing, food and access to him by bringing them into Egypt with him!

Your Assignment will bring someone great joy.

So, be willing to face your enemy. Confront your critics.

Endure the season of overload.

Your own Assignment may not appear to be very significant at this time. Your mind may be a whirlpool of options and choices to make. You may toss and turn at night, wondering how you are going to feed your own children and make your car payment. Begin completing the Assignment closest to your heart. Listen carefully to the Holy Spirit.

Each act of obedience will create a new wave of blessing around you. Those you love will reap ten thousand times from your obedience to God.

Seasons *change.* Your present season may be extremely difficult. It may seem to stretch every fiber of your being. You may even feel like giving up, quitting and walking away from your Assignment. Do not do it. Joy is too close to give up now! "Weeping may endure for a night, but joy cometh in the morning" (Psalm 30:5).

Remember: *Your Assignment Will Bring Someone Great Joy.*

Delayed Obedience
Is Disobedience.

-MIKE MURDOCK

≈ 43 ≈

IF YOU REBEL AGAINST YOUR ASSIGNMENT, YOU EXPOSE YOUR ENTIRE FAMILY TO POSSIBLE LOSS AND TRAGEDY.

Everything You Do Is A Seed.

Your obedience will create waves of *blessing.*

Your *disobedience* will create waves of pain. The Word of God confirms this truth. "If ye be willing and obedient, ye shall eat the good of the land: But if ye refuse and rebel, ye shall be devoured with the sword: for the mouth of the Lord hath spoken it" (Isaiah 1:19,20).

My father has always had a deep fear of offending God. So, I was taught this principle through the Word of God and through my father. To this very day, I have never heard my father utter a negative remark against any man of God. Some have wronged him. Some have embarrassed him publicly. Yet my father would never raise his hand or his voice against them.

There is a guaranteed reaction from God against anyone who touches His anointed. My father always believed that. "Who art thou that judgest another man's servant? to his own master he standeth or falleth" (Romans 14:4). As my mother would always say, "They will have to give an account of themselves before God."

Disobedience always produces pain. There is an interesting story in the Old Testament where Korah and 250 members of his family rebelled against Moses, the Man of God. They refused to follow the man God had assigned over their life. Korah was a rebel. He did not like Moses' leadership. He disagreed with his decisions. Instead of quietly entering the prayer closet, and pouring out his heart to God, he stirred up opposition to Moses.

He refused to focus on his Assignment of supporting the man of God.

His entire family paid dearly for his rebellion.

God opened up the earth and destroyed them. When many of his friends came to Moses and complained the next day, the wrath of God went forth *again*. The plague broke out among them and killed more than 14,000 (see Numbers 16:1-35).

If you refuse to carry out your Assignment, your entire family may be ushered into a season of tragedies. Stay faithful to God. Stay faithful to your Assignment. Too much is at stake. Too many miracles are ahead. Too much pain can be produced through a single act of disobedience.

Remember: *If You Rebel Against Your Assignment, You Expose Your Entire Family To Possible Loss And Tragedy.*

⟫ 44 ⟪

YOUR ASSIGNMENT WILL ALWAYS INVOLVE SEASONS OF SERVANTHOOD.

Every Successful Person Has Served Someone Very Well.

13 Facts About Servanthood

1. *Jesus Taught Servanthood.* He made a fascinating statement: "The disciple is not above his master, nor the servant above his Lord" (Matthew 10:24).

2. *Joseph Excelled In Servanthood.* First, he served Potiphar. Then, when he was falsely accused by his master's wife and thrown into jail, he served in the prison until he became the head. When he was released and promoted, he then served Pharaoh as prime minister of the nation.

Joshua served Moses. Esther served the king. Jonathan served David. Elisha served Elijah. Ruth served Naomi.

3. *Servanthood Is The Golden Gate To Uncommon Promotion.* There is a reason for the chain of authority.

There is a reason for obedience. The purpose of supervision is not restraint, but promotion.

4. *You Can Only Be Promoted By Someone Whose Instructions You Have Followed.*

When God established the chain of authority, He was not trying to restrict, restrain and confine you. He was not trying to stop your flexibility, destroy your creativity and imprison you.

5. *Whoever God Has Assigned Over You Becomes Qualified To Promote You.* That is the purpose of accountability.

6. *Someone Is Qualified As The Golden Connection To Move You From Where You Are To Where You Should Be.*

7. *God Has Called You To Serve Someone.* Who are they? *Where* are they? *How* can you serve them better? With what kind of *attitude and spirit* do you serve them?

Serve with diligence. Diligence is immediate attention to an assigned task.

8. *The Uncommon Employee Will Increase His Personal Wealth And The Money Of His Boss.* "The hand of the diligent maketh rich" (Proverbs 10:4).

9. *The Uncommon Employee Will Always Rise To The Position Of Supervisor.* "The hand of the diligent shall bear rule:" (Proverbs 12:24).

10. *The Uncommon Employee Uses Everything God Has Given Him.* "The slothful man roasteh not that which he took in hunting: but the substance of a diligent man is precious" (Proverbs 12:27).

11. *The Uncommon Employee Will Always Prosper.* "...the soul of the diligent shall be made fat" (Proverbs 13:4).

12. *The Focus Of The Uncommon Employee Is On Increasing The Success Of His Boss.* "The thoughts of the diligent tend only to plenteousness;" (Proverbs 21:5).

13. *The Uncommon Employee Will Always Be Pursued By Uncommon Leaders.* "Seest thou a man diligent in his business? he shall stand before kings; he shall not stand before mean men" (Proverbs 22:29).

Remember: *Your Assignment Will Always Involve Seasons Of Servanthood.*

⇒ 45 ⇐

THOSE WHO UNLOCK YOUR COMPASSION ARE OFTEN THOSE TO WHOM YOU ARE ASSIGNED.

⇒➤◦◉◦◄⇐

Compassion Is The Intense Desire To Heal The Hurting.

Someone has said, "Compassion is the irresistible urge to rid a problem for someone."

6 Facts You Should Know About The Force Of Compassion

1. *Jesus Had Great Compassion Toward The Sick.* "And Jesus, moved with compassion, put forth His hand, and touched him, and saith unto him, I will; be thou clean. And as soon as He had spoken, immediately the leprosy departed from him, and he was cleansed" (Mark 1:41,42).

Compassion *moves* toward someone.

Compassion *restores* the broken.

Compassion *heals*.

2. *Jesus Had Compassion Toward Those Who Were Spiritually Confused, Wasted And Bewildered.* "And Jesus, when He came out, saw much people, and was moved with compassion toward them, because they were as sheep not having a shepherd: and He began to teach them many things" (Mark 6:34).

Compassion *discerns* the wounded.

Compassion causes you to *reach*.

Compassion births *feelings*.

3. *Compassion Can Preserve A Life.* It did for Moses when he was just a baby. "And the daughter of Pharaoh came down to wash herself at the river; and her maidens walked along by the river's side; and when she saw the ark among the flags, she sent her maid to fetch it. And when she had opened it, she saw the child: and, behold, the babe wept. And she had compassion on

him, and said, This is one of the Hebrews' children" (Exodus 2:5,6).

4. *Those Who Unlock Your Compassion Are Those To Whom You Have Been Assigned.* Whose *pain* do you feel today? Whose tears do you long to wipe away? Whose sorrows keep you awake at night? This kind of compassion restores, repairs and revitalizes the life of someone close to you.

5. *Your Compassion Affects The Destiny Of Others.* "Keep yourselves in the love of God, looking for the mercy of our Lord Jesus Christ unto eternal life. And of some have compassion, making a difference: And others save with fear, pulling them out of the fire;" (Jude 1:21-23).

6. *Expect The Holy Spirit To Impart Uncommon Compassion For Your Assignment.* Strongly resist complacency. Ask the Holy Spirit for a special compassion for those to whom you are assigned. He will give it to you. "Brethren, if a man be overtaken in a fault, ye which are spiritual, restore such an one in the spirit of meekness; considering thyself, lest thou also be tempted. Bear ye one another's burdens, and so fulfil the law of Christ" (Galatians 6:1,2).

Remember: *Those Who Unlock Your Compassion Are Often Those To Whom You Are Assigned.*

～ 46 ～

AN UNCOMMON ASSIGNMENT WILL REQUIRE UNCOMMON PASSION.

━━━━►▷◦◁◄━━━━

Passion Is Desire.

It includes the desire to change, serve or achieve a goal.

Men who succeed greatly possess great passion for their Assignment. They are consumed and obsessed. It burns within them like fire. Nothing else matters to them but the completion of the instructions of God in their lives.

Isaiah was passionate. "For the Lord God will help me; therefore shall I not be confounded: therefore have I set my face like a flint, and I know that I shall not be ashamed" (Isaiah 50:7).

The Apostle Paul was passionate. "Brethren, I count not myself to have apprehended: but this one thing I do, forgetting those things which are behind, and reaching forth unto those things which are before, I press toward the mark for the prize of the high calling of God in Christ Jesus" (Philippians 3:13,14).

Jesus was passionate about completing and finishing His Assignment on earth. "Looking unto Jesus the Author and Finisher of our faith; Who for the joy that was set before Him endured the cross, despising the shame, and is set down at the right hand of the throne of God. For consider Him that endured such contradiction of sinners against Himself, lest ye be wearied and faint in your minds" (Hebrews 12:2,3).

You are instructed to develop a passion for the Word of God. The Lord spoke to Joshua about the Law and instructed him to "turn not from it to the right hand or to the left, that thou mayest prosper whithersoever thou goest. This book of the law shall not depart out of thy mouth; but thou shalt meditate therein day and night, that thou mayest observe to do according to all that is written therein: for then thou shalt make thy way prosperous, and then thou shalt have good success" (Joshua 1:7,8).

So, move toward His presence today. Habitually schedule time in The Secret Place. "He that dwelleth in The Secret Place of the most High shall abide under the shadow of the Almighty" (Psalm 91:1). In His presence, your passion for Him will grow from a tiny acorn to a huge oak within you.

Wrong relationships will weaken your passion for your Assignment for God. Recently, I went to dinner with several friends after a service. Within one hour, the discussion had become filled with the problems with people, financial difficulties and complaining attitudes. I was shocked at what began to grow within me. Though I had left the service with great joy, something began to die within me. As others discussed the difficult situations in their lives or how difficult it was to reach their goals, I felt my own fire begin to go out. Paul warned of such associations. "Be not deceived: evil communications corrupt good manners" (1 Corinthians 15:33).

Protect the Gift of Passion within you. Guard your focus every hour. Be ruthless with distractions. Feed the picture of your goal continually. Watch for the Four Enemies of Passion: fatigue, busyness, overscheduling and putting God last on your daily schedule.

Remember: *An Uncommon Assignment Will Require Uncommon Passion.*

❧ 47 ❧

YOUR ASSIGNMENT WILL REQUIRE SEASONS OF SUBMISSION TO SOMEONE.

You Must Serve Somebody.

Submission is the most misunderstood doctrine of the entire Bible.

Here Are 25 Powerful Facts About Submission

1. *Submission Is The Willingness To Embrace The Leadership Of Those Responsible For Governing Our Lives.*

2. *You Are Commanded To Submit To The Word Of God And The Chain Of Authority It Teaches.* The Scriptures are "...able to make thee wise unto salvation through faith which is in Christ Jesus...That the man of God may be perfect, throughly furnished unto all good works" (2 Timothy 3:15,17). "If ye be willing and obedient, ye shall eat the good of the land:" (Isaiah 1:19).

3. *Submission Is A Personal Choice.* "God resisteth the proud, but giveth grace unto the humble. Humble yourselves in the sight of the Lord, and He shall lift you up" (James 4:6,10).

4. *Submission Reveals Humility.* Some people assume that leadership is strength, and submission implies weakness. However, true submission is evidence of flexibility, trust and humility. It is the quality of champions.

Submission is proof of humility. Humility is the gate to promotion. "Humble yourselves therefore under the mighty hand of God, that He may exalt you in due time:" (1 Peter 5:6).

5. *Submission Is Your Personal Gift Of Cooperation To Those Who Govern You.* Every great leader began as a great follower. They honored authority established by God. "Obey them that have the rule over you, and submit yourselves: for they watch for your souls, as they that must give account, that they may do it with joy,

and not with grief: for that *is* unprofitable for you" (Hebrews 13:17). It was *not* their weakness that made them easy to govern. Rather, it was their deep *understanding* of the laws of promotion. "Seest thou a man diligent in his business? He shall stand before kings; he shall not stand before mean men" (Proverbs 22:29).

6. *Jesus Himself Knew The Rewards Of Submission.* When He prayed in the Garden of Gethsemane, He prayed this prayer before Calvary. "O My Father, if it be possible, let this cup pass from Me: nevertheless not as I will, but as Thou wilt" (Matthew 26:39).

7. *Submission Always Results In Inner Joy.* "Looking unto Jesus the Author and Finisher of our faith; Who for the joy that was set before Him endured the cross, despising the shame, and is set down at the right hand of the throne of God" (Hebrews 12:2).

8. *Elisha Obeyed And Submitted To His Mentor, Elijah.* He received a double portion of Elijah's anointing as a reward.

9. *Those Who Refuse To Submit To The Chain Of Authority Experience Seasons Of Tragedy.* "But if ye refuse and rebel, ye shall be devoured with the sword: for the mouth of the Lord hath spoken it" (Isaiah 1:20).

10. *Submission To The Spirit Of God Produces Prosperity.* "And he sought God in the days of Zechariah, who had understanding in the visions of God: and as long as he sought the Lord, God made him to prosper" (2 Chronicles 26:5).

11. *Prosperity Always Follows Submission To An Instruction From A True Man Or Woman Of God.* "Believe in the Lord your God, so shall ye be established; believe His prophets, so shall ye prosper" (2 Chronicles 20:20).

12. *The Word Of God Commands Submission To Wise And Qualified Spiritual Leadership.* "Remember them which have the rule over you, who have spoken unto you the Word of God: whose faith follow, considering the end of their conversation" (Hebrews 13:7).

13. *Children Are Commanded To Submit To Parents.* The Apostle Paul emphasizes this. "Children, obey your parents in the Lord: for this is right. Honour thy father and mother; which is the first commandment with promise; That it may be well with thee, and thou mayest live long on the earth" (Ephesians 6:1-3). Longevity is promised. Health is promised. "Children, obey your parents in all things: for this is well pleasing unto the Lord"

(Colossians 3:20).

14. *Submission To Parental Authority Guarantees Lifetime Blessing.* "Honour thy father and thy mother: that thy days may be long upon the land which the Lord thy God giveth thee" (Exodus 20:12).

15. *Fathers Must Submit To The Standard Of The Word Of God In Rearing Their Children.* Fathers are instructed, "...provoke not your children to wrath: but bring them up in the nurture and admonition of the Lord" (Ephesians 6:4).

16. *Wives Are Instructed To Submit Themselves To The Spiritual Authority Of Their Husbands.* "Wives, submit yourselves unto your own husbands, as unto the Lord. For the husband is the head of the wife, even as Christ is the head of the church: and He is the saviour of the body. Therefore as the church is subject unto Christ, so let the wives be to their own husbands in every thing" (Ephesians 5:22-24).

17. *Employees Are Instructed To Have A Submissive Attitude Toward Their Bosses.* "Servants, be obedient to them that are your masters according to the flesh, with fear and trembling, in singleness of your heart, as unto Christ; Not with eyeservice, as menpleasers; but as the servants of Christ, doing the will of God from the heart; With good will doing service, as to the Lord, and not to men:" (Ephesians 6:5-7). God guarantees then, that what you make happen for others, He will make happen for you. "Knowing that whatsoever good thing any man doeth, the same shall he receive of the Lord, whether he be bond or free" (Ephesians 6:8).

18. *The Word Of God Commands Our Submission In Honoring And Respecting One Another.* "Submitting yourselves one to another in the fear of God" (Ephesians 5:21). "Whosoever therefore shall humble himself as this little child, the same is greatest in the kingdom of heaven" (Matthew 18:4).

19. *Humble Submission Guarantees Uncommon Provision.* "By humility and the fear of the Lord are riches, and honour, and life" (Proverbs 22:4).

20. *The Scriptures Document Those Rewarded For Submission.* Ruth was submissive to Naomi. Ruth told her, "...whither thou goest, I will go; and where thou lodgest, I will lodge: thy people shall be my people, and thy God my God: Where thou diest, will I die, and there will I be buried: the Lord do so to

me, and more also, if ought but death part thee and me" (Ruth 1:16,17). It was her Golden Link to Boaz, the provider and husband of her life.

21. *Your Submission To Authority Is Often Reproduced In Those Who Serve You.* David honored Saul, king of Israel. Likewise, his own men proved to be incredibly loyal and steadfast in following him. *What you are, you will create around you.* When you submit to those over you, it motivates those under *your* rule to submit to you as well. You become their example.

22. *The Submission Of Parents To Authority Directly Affects The Behavior Of Their Children.* Just a brief note to parents: When your child sees a radar detector on the dash of your car, it is a monument to your personal rebellion to law. It will be almost impossible to persuade your children to submit to your government and authority when you obviously have no respect for law and authority over your own life.

23. *Joshua Was Loyal And Submissive To Moses.* The Israelites observed this. It affected them after the death of Moses. They spoke to Joshua, "And they answered Joshua, saying, All that thou commandest us we will do, and whithersoever thou sendest us, we will go. According as we hearkened unto Moses in all things, so will we hearken unto thee: only the Lord thy God be with thee, as He was with Moses" (Joshua 1:16,17).

24. *Employers Are Instructed To Submit To The Authority And Standards Of God.* "And, ye masters, do the same things unto them, forbearing threatening: knowing that your Master also is in heaven; neither is there respect of persons with Him" (Ephesians 6:9).

25. *Those Who Govern You Are Under The Authority Of God As Well.* Husbands are commanded to treat their wives as Christ treated the church. "Husbands, love your wives, even as Christ also loved the church, and gave Himself for it;...So ought men to love their wives as their own bodies. He that loveth his wife loveth himself. For no man ever yet hated his own flesh; but nourisheth and cherisheth it, even as the Lord the church:" (Ephesians 5:25,28,29).

Remember: *Your Assignment Will Require Seasons Of Submission To Someone.*

❧ 48 ❧

GOD OFTEN USES SOMEONE IN AUTHORITY OVER YOU TO ADVANCE YOUR ASSIGNMENT.

Authority Is *Not* Permission To *Dominate*.

Authority *is* permission to *promote*.

The purpose of authority is not merely to restrict, but rather to advance another, to recognize and reward their obedience.

Authority requires qualification.

Authority Should Offer 3 Rewards To Those Who Decide To Cooperate, Obey, Follow Or Submit

1. *Qualified Authority Should Offer Protection To You.* God did for Israel. "And I will rebuke the devourer for your sakes, and he shall not destroy the fruits of your ground; neither shall your vine cast her fruit before the time in the field, saith the Lord of hosts" (Malachi 3:11).

Note that God did not simply instruct us to bring the tithe to Him. He promised to *protect* everything we create and generate. The covenant rewards everyone involved.

Fathers are commanded to *protect their families* and children, not merely to give them instructions and commands.

Ministers are commanded to *protect their flock,* not simply to instruct them to bring offerings to Sunday morning services.

Counselors provide protection. "Where no counsel is, the people fall: but in the multitude of counsellors there is safety" (Proverbs 11:14).

The government that requires taxes is then obligated to provide *military protection* for its citizens. If it is permissible for the government to tax my property, then the government should provide quality highways and roads.

2. *Qualified Authority Should Produce Provision For You.* That is exactly what God promised. "If thou shalt hearken diligently unto the voice of the Lord thy God, to observe and to do all His commandments which I command thee this day, The Lord shall command the blessing upon thee in thy storehouses, and in all that thou settest thine hand unto; And the Lord shall make thee plenteous in goods, in the fruit of thy body, and in the fruit of thy cattle, and in the fruit of thy ground, The Lord shall open unto thee His good treasure, the heaven to give the rain unto thy land in His season, and to bless all the work of thine hand: thou shalt lend unto many nations and thou shalt not borrow" (Deuteronomy 28:1,8,11,12).

Fathers are commanded to produce financial provision. It is important that the father who enjoys headship of his family also remembers he is required by God to provide financially for every member of that family. "But if any provide not for his own, and specially for those of his own house, he hath denied the faith, and is worse than an infidel" (1 Timothy 5:8).

Ministers are commanded to produce spiritual provision. Ministers, it is not enough for you to receive the offerings and tithes of the people. You are required by God to be the *spiritual* provider in their life. "Should not the shepherds feed the flocks? Ye eat the fat, and ye clothe you with the wool, ye kill them that are fed: but ye feed not the flock. The diseased have ye not strengthened, neither have ye healed that which was sick, neither have ye bound up that which was broken, neither have ye brought again that which was driven away, neither have ye sought that which was lost; but with force and with cruelty have ye ruled them. And they were scattered, because there is no shepherd: and they became meat to all the beasts of the field, when they were scattered. My sheep wandered through all the mountains, and upon every high hill: yea, my flock was scattered upon all the face of the earth, and none did search or seek after them" (Ezekiel 34:2-6).

3. *Qualified Authority Should Promote You.* Obviously, the true source of every promotion is God, Who honors a broken and

contrite spirit. "The sacrifices of God are a broken spirit: a broken and a contrite heart, O God, Thou wilt not despise" (Psalm 51:17).

"For promotion cometh neither from the east, nor from the west, nor from the south. But God is the judge: He putteth down one, and setteth up another" (Psalm 75:6,7).

Those who rule over you are instructed to reward you. "Withhold not good from them to whom it is due, when it is in the power of thine hand to do it" (Proverbs 3:27).

Submission is always rewarded, when it is according to the Word of God.

So, your Assignment will contain many different seasons. Do not be weary when you feel stressed, overwhelmed and incapable of meeting the requirements of others. "And let us not be weary in well doing: for in due season we shall reap, if we faint not" (Galatians 6:9).

Reaping days are coming. They will be the greatest days of your life.

Remember: *God Often Uses Someone In Authority Over You To Advance Your Assignment.*

The Quality Of A Nation
Is Revealed By The Leader
God Permits To Govern It.

-MIKE MURDOCK

≈ 49 ≈

ANY LEADER WHO WILLFULLY HINDERS YOUR ASSIGNMENT WILL BE JUDGED BY GOD.

God Sees Everything.

God will judge cruel spiritual leadership. "Thus saith the Lord God; Behold, I am against the shepherds; and I will require My flock at their hand, and cause them to cease from feeding the flock; neither shall the shepherds feed themselves any more; for I will deliver My flock from their mouth, that they may not be meat for them" (Ezekiel 34:10).

I have a wonderful word for you who have experienced cruel rulership at the hands of a spiritual despot or tyrant: God is coming toward you today. He will not leave you damaged and broken in the hands of a cruel father, husband or spiritual leader. This is what He promised:

▶ Behold, I, even I, will both search My sheep, and seek them out. As a shepherd seeketh out his flock in the day that he is among his sheep that are scattered; so will I seek out My sheep, and will deliver them out of all places where they have been scattered in the cloudy and dark day.

▶ And I will bring them out from the people, and gather them from the countries, and will bring them to their own land, and feed them upon the mountains of Israel by the rivers, and in all the inhabited places of the country.

▶ I will feed them in a good pasture, and upon the high mountains of Israel shall their fold be: there shall they lie in a good fold, and in a fat pasture shall they feed upon the mountains of Israel.

▶ I will feed My flock, and I will cause them to lie down, saith the Lord God.

▶ I will seek that which was lost, and bring again that which was driven away, and will bind up that which was broken, and will strengthen that which was sick: (Ezekiel 34:11-16).

Never follow unqualified leadership. It is possible that teachings about submission have left a bitter taste in your mouth. I have experienced that in my personal life. I have known men who were in authority over me who never took the time to hear my cries, dry my tears and heal my wounds. It birthed bitterness at various seasons of my personal life and ministry.

I experienced a broken marriage many years ago. It was quite interesting to observe that men who wanted me to tithe from my ministry to their organization, never telephoned me, wrote me or came to my court hearing. They merely wanted to rule me and extract from me financially and emotionally. Yet, when I was devastated and left on the road, they refused to become The Good Samaritan in my life.

They disqualified themselves to rule over me.

I am so thankful that I experienced the precious visitation and companionship of the Holy Spirit. I have learned so much in submitting to Him on a daily and hourly basis. Jesus prayed to the Father, and the Father asked the Holy Spirit to come. The Holy Spirit accommodated both the desires of the Son and the Father. That kind of ministry attitude is the force that brings reward, promotion and provision from God.

Stop for a moment. Reconsider the direction you are going with your life. *Make a quality decision to follow quality leadership around you.* When you do, you will experience the supernatural one-hundredfold blessing that Jesus promised (see Mark 10:28-30).

Your best days are ahead as you yield to the authority of God and spiritual leadership in your life. Walls of protection will be built by the Holy Spirit around your life. Your children will rise up to call you blessed. Those who rule over you will promote and reward you. You will taste the greatest chapters you have ever known in the coming days. God *promised* it. "And I will make them and the places round about My hill a blessing; and I will cause the shower to come down in his season; there shall be showers of blessing. And the tree of the field shall yield her fruit, and the earth shall yield her increase, and they shall be safe in their land, and shall know that I am the Lord," (Ezekiel 34:26,27).

Remember: *Any Leader Who Willfully Hinders Your Assignment Will Be Judged By God.*

When Wrong People
Enter Your Life
Wrong Things
Start Happening.

-MIKE MURDOCK

∽ 50 ∽

YOUR ASSIGNMENT MAY ATTRACT PEOPLE WITH WRONG MOTIVES.

━━━◦━

Pursuers Always Have A Motive.
Sometimes, it is pure. Sometimes, it is not!
Whatever it is, uncover it.

When someone shows warmth and kindness at an unexpected time, it often strengthens us. It makes us feel special, celebrated and treasured. But I have learned through difficult times that when someone is excessively congenial toward you, there is sometimes a hidden and impure motive behind it.

It happened to me a few days ago. An urgent telephone call came. Since I had not heard from this friend in almost two years, I decided to make his telephone call a priority. I accepted the call.

"Hello, Mike! I just had you on my mind for the last two weeks. I was just wondering how your ministry is going. How are you doing? Where have you been?"

As he spoke, my mind was moving swiftly. Why is he calling me just to ask me about my ministry? He has never sown one single cent into my ministry. He never writes. He has not attended one of my services in more than seven years. Why this sudden *deluge* of friendliness? I kept listening. Then, I decided to end the conversation because I had an incredible list of things to do before leaving for a crusade.

He interrupted me. "Oh, I just wanted to mention something to you." When he finished, I felt stupid, taken and had. He simply wanted me to give some money to one of his friends. In fact, he wanted me to give a large amount of money to them for a project I knew nothing about. Absolutely nothing.

This may sound peculiar, but I absolutely felt dirty, a bit sick inside. Something inside me never wanted to hear from him again. You see, he was not genuinely interested in my ministry. He used the warm words to set me up.

It occurs quite often in life. You must confront it honestly. Name it for what it is.

Recently a well-known personality kept telephoning. He had not called me in years. And, he had never called without a reason, a motive. He gushed with praise of my ministry and work. I listened intently. "I need to meet and talk to you face to face." Something told me inside what it was. And, I was not wrong. He was involved in a multi-level marketing program, and wanted my involvement and influence.

"You know *everybody*. I could make you a fortune," he said excitedly.

He never pursued an understanding of my anointing, mantle or Assignment. Not once did he ask me what he could do to help me reach my own goals and dreams. He had his own agenda. I explained that my obsession was knowing the Holy Spirit. The Secret Place had become my focus. I wanted to spend the rest of my life writing in books what the Holy Spirit was teaching me in The Secret Place.

I have not received a phone call from him since.

Many years ago, someone rushed up to me after a conference. They were syrupy, full of flattery and warm words. I did not know them at all. But, within thirty minutes, the motive appeared.

"I understand that you sponsored a music album for a friend of mine!"

"Yes, I did," I replied slowly. "It was $25,000 cash from my pocket," I said. "It was a Seed into their ministry."

"Well, I would like for you to do the same thing for me! I want to make an album. It is my life-long dream. Could you give me $25,000?"

I sat there stunned. What kind of audacity and boldness is this? How brassy can people become?

There was not one mention of even borrowing the money and repaying it. They wanted it. They thought I had it. So, "give it to me."

Always be cautious concerning the hidden agendas of those

who pursue you.
> ▶ "Meddle not with him that flattereth with his lips" (Proverbs 20:19).
> ▶ "A man that flattereth his neighbour spreadeth a net for his feet" (Proverbs 29:5).
> ▶ "The Lord shall cut off all flattering lips," (Psalm 12:3).
> ▶ "A flattering mouth worketh ruin" (Proverbs 26:28).

The Apostle Paul despised flattering words and wrong motives. "For neither at any time used we flattering words, as ye know, Nor of men sought we glory, neither of you, nor yet of others, when we might have been burdensome, as the apostles of Christ. But we were gentle among you, even as a nurse cherisheth her children:" (1 Thessalonians 2:5-7).

I have had quite a bit of exposure in the area of gospel music. Because I know artists who record songs, it has been a normal occurrence to have someone shove cassettes and sheet music into my hands and say, "God told me that you are my connection to this artist. Will you see that they receive this and tell them about me?" This has occurred on many occasions.

Now, I am a musician. I am a song writer. So, I understand the desire for others to sing my songs. But, my Assignment to help people has attracted some with *wrong* motives. It is my personal responsibility to test, qualify and discern their true intent and motives.

It happened to Peter and John. Read the complete fascinating story in Acts 8. Simon, who had practiced sorcery "...himself believed also: and when he was baptized, he continued with Philip, and wondered, beholding the miracles and signs which were done" (Acts 8:13).

But, wrong motives entered.

"And when Simon saw that through laying on of the apostles' hands the Holy Ghost was given, he offered them money, Saying, Give me also this power, that on whomsoever I lay hands, he may receive the Holy Ghost" (Acts 8:18,19).

Peter had discerned Simon's wrong motive. "For I perceive that thou art in the gall of bitterness, and in the bond of iniquity" (Acts 8:23).

Peter reacted to wrong motives in a strong, decisive and

dramatic way. "But Peter said unto him, Thy money perish with thee, because thou hast thought that the gift of God may be purchased with money. Thou hast neither part nor lot in this matter: for thy heart is not right in the sight of God. Repent therefore of this thy wickedness, and pray God, if perhaps the thought of thine heart may be forgiven thee" (Acts 8:20-22).

After a crusade service one night, my assistant handed me a business card. It was from a wealthy man with a very successful business. My assistant explained, "He has heard about the results of your prayers for the prosperity of Christian business people. He has heard of your anointing with oil the door posts of businesses, and asking God's blessing upon that place. He pulled out a huge stack of money and wanted me to give it to you if you would come pray over his business."

"You know that I will not do that," was my reply.

"I told him that. He said you could name your price, and he would pay you whatever you want, to pray over his business."

I threw the card away.

My prayers are not "for sale."

My faith will not be prostituted.

My confidence in God cannot be merchandised.

If there is an anointing that flows through your life, it will have a *magnetism.* Unfortunately, it often attracts wrong people as well as deserving individuals.

You may have a special mantle of financial blessing on your life. Perhaps, you are a paymaster for the kingdom, one of those persons who God touches and causes great wealth to flow through your hands to touch many lives. It is important that you understand the magnetism, appeal and drawing power your money has with many. One of the wealthiest men who ever lived wrote, "The poor is hated even of his own neighbour: but the rich hath many friends" (Proverbs 14:20). He insisted again, "Wealth maketh many friends; but the poor is separated from his neighbour" (Proverbs 19:4).

During the last several years, I have received letters from various ministers, musicians and aggressive achievers who wrote me, "I would like for you to recommend me to be on this particular television show. I know they are friends of yours. Would you introduce me?"

When I failed to respond, I never heard from them again. To them, I was merely a "stepping stone" on the way to their future.

Please understand, I *love* sowing into the lives of worthy people. I *love* giving. It is a powerful part of my nature. In fact, I give away thousands of books and tapes each month. It is a Law of Blessing. Jesus guaranteed one hundredfold return for anything given up for the sake of the gospel (see Mark 10:28-30).

The giving of gifts can even conceal hidden agendas. Unfortunately, satan has often used giving as a weapon of manipulation. It happened some months ago. I suddenly received in the mail a very expensive and exquisite gift from someone who had never written me, never given me anything, nor attended my meetings. I pondered on this.

A few weeks later, my secretary approached me and said, "You received a telephone call from someone who wants to meet with you." I realized that the purpose of the gift was to soften me up for the meeting. This is unfortunate. It is ungodly. It is wrong. "A wicked man taketh a gift out of the bosom to pervert the ways of judgment" (Proverbs 17:23).

When a gift is given from a pure heart to honor another, it prospers the relationship. It prospers the *sower.* It prospers the one who *receives.* "A gift *is as* a precious stone in the eyes of him that hath it: whithersoever it turneth, it prospereth" (Proverbs 17:8).

Motives should *strengthen* relationships.

Motives should *build* bridges.

Motives should *reveal* caring, compassion and appreciation.

Remember: *Your Assignment May Attract People With Wrong Motives.*

Your Reaction
To A Man Of God
Determines
God's Reaction To You.

-MIKE MURDOCK

≈ 51 ≈

THOSE WHO SCORN YOUR ASSIGNMENT MAY SUFFER DEVASTATING LOSSES.

Your Assignment Is Serious To God.

It should become serious to others. God will hold them accountable for their reaction to it.

Those who scorned the Apostle Peter's ministry suffered tragedy. Let me explain. Ananias and Sapphira lost their lives after lying to Peter. It was a loss that was unnecessary and avoidable. They simply should have told the truth (read Acts 5:1-11).

Those who rally opposition to spiritual leaders expose their family to the wrath of God. Korah and his family were destroyed by God when they acted in rebellion against the authority of Moses. It was avoidable. They should have been teachable. The tragedy could have been averted (read Numbers 16:1-40).

Those unoffended by sin may eventually lose their ability to experience correction. Lot's wife looked back. She became a pillar of salt. That was avoidable and unnecessary. She kept her ties to the ungodly in Sodom and Gomorrah (see Genesis 19:26).

Those who knowingly attempt to lie to a man of God will open the floodgates of hell against their life. Gehazi, the servant of Elisha the man of God, had a horrifying experience. It followed the healing of Naaman, the leper. Naaman wanted to bless Elisha, the man of God. After Elisha turned down the gift, Gehazi discreetly went to Naaman and asked for the gift. When he returned, Elisha knew in his heart what Gehazi had done. Gehazi lied when Elisha interrogated him about his whereabouts. Elisha pronounced his penalty. "The leprosy therefore of Naaman shall cleave unto thee, and unto thy seed for ever. And he went out from his presence a leper as white as snow" (2 Kings 5:27).

The assistant to the prophet lost his position, his health and his credibility. It was unnecessary and totally avoidable. He could have simply told the truth.

Remember: *Those Who Scorn Your Assignment May Suffer Devastating Losses.*

❧ 52 ❧

OBEDIENCE TO YOUR ASSIGNMENT MAY CREATE A TEMPORARY SEASON OF LOSS.

————⊱•◦•⊰————

Some Losses Are Avoidable.

Some losses are vital.

Obedience is rarely easy.

Yet, your Assignment will require many acts of obedience. Some of those instructions will create losses. However, those losses are necessary and essential for long term gains. God has *reasons* for every demand He makes upon your life.

Moses experienced the loss of status and position. "By faith Moses, when he was come to years, refused to be called the son of Pharaoh's daughter; Choosing rather to suffer affliction with the people of God, than to enjoy the pleasures of sin for a season; Esteeming the reproach of Christ greater riches than the treasures in Egypt: for he had respect unto the recompense of the reward. By faith he forsook Egypt, not fearing the wrath of the king: for he endured, as seeing him who is invisible" (Hebrews 11:24-27).

Moses saw the *bigger* picture. He saw the future. He saw the *reward*. He knew the limitations of Egypt. He knew the inevitable eventuality of *promotion*. "And let us not be weary in well doing: for in due season we shall reap, if we faint not" (Galatians 6:9).

You see, seasons change.

"To every thing there is a season, and a time to every purpose under the heaven: A time to be born, and a time to die; a time to plant, and a time to pluck up that which is planted; A time to kill, and a time to heal; a time to break down, and a time to build up; A time to weep, and a time to laugh; a time to mourn, and a time to dance; A time to cast away stones, and a time to gather stones together; a time to embrace, and a time to refrain from embracing; A time to get, and a time to lose; a time to keep, and a time to cast away;" (Ecclesiastes 3:1-6).

Abraham knew the losses of comfort, friends and home. "Now the Lord had said unto Abram, Get thee out of thy country, and from thy kindred, and from thy father's house, unto a land that I will shew thee:" (Genesis 12:1).

Abraham was tested with the potential loss of his son of promise, Isaac. "And it came to pass after these things, that God did tempt Abraham, and said unto him, Abraham: and he said, Behold, here I am. And he said, Take now thy son, thine only son Isaac, whom thou lovest, and get thee into the land of Moriah; and offer him there for a burnt offering upon one of the mountains which I will tell thee of" (Genesis 22:1,2).

Abraham knew the loss of peaceful relationships. "And Lot also, which went with Abram, had flocks, and herds, and tents. And the land was not able to bear them, that they might dwell together: for their substance was great, so that they could not dwell together. And there was a strife between the herdmen of Abram's cattle and the herdmen of Lot's cattle: and the Canaanite and the Perizzite dwelled then in the land. And Abram said unto Lot, Let there be no strife, I pray thee, between me and thee, and between my herdmen and thy herdmen; for we be brethren. Is not the whole land before thee? Separate thyself, I pray thee, from me: if thou wilt take the left hand, then I will go to the right; or if thou depart to the right hand, then I will go to the left" (Genesis 13:5-9).

Abraham persisted in serving God through seasons of loss. "He staggered not at the promise of God through unbelief; but was strong in faith, giving glory to God; And being fully persuaded that, what He had promised, He was able also to perform" (Romans 4:20,21).

Abraham was rewarded for every loss. He became the Father of Nations. "Therefore it is of faith, that it might be by grace; to the end the promise might be sure to all the seed; not to that only which is of the law, but to that also which is of the faith of Abraham; who is the father of us all, (As it is written, I have made thee a father of many nations,) before Him Whom he believed, even God, Who quickeneth the dead, and calleth those things which be not as though they were. Who against hope believed in hope, that he might become the father of many nations, according to that which was spoken, So shall thy seed be" (Romans 4:16-18).

Stephen lost his life. I find the story of Stephen fascinating. He was the first minister of help selected by the early church. The widows were neglected. The twelve disciples asked the multitude to select seven men to handle the business of the church. The first they chose was "Stephen, a man full of faith and of the Holy Ghost, And Stephen, full of faith and power, did great wonders and miracles among the people" (Acts 6:5,8).

When Stephen spoke, conviction was so powerful that men responded with anger. "And they were not able to resist the wisdom and the Spirit by which he spake" (Acts 6:10).

When people saw Stephen, his countenance was like an angel. "And all that sat in the council, looking steadfastly on him, saw his face as it had been the face of an angel" (Acts 6:15).

Overwhelmed with conviction, they decided to kill him. "When they heard these things, they were cut to the heart, and they gnashed on him with their teeth. Then they cried out with a loud voice, and stopped their ears, and ran upon him with one accord, and cast him out of the city, and stoned him: And they stoned Stephen, calling upon God, and saying, Lord Jesus, receive my spirit" (Acts 7:54,57-59).

Yes, he lost his life.

But look at what happened. "But he, being full of the Holy Ghost, looked up stedfastly into heaven, and saw the glory of God, and Jesus standing on the right hand of God. And he kneeled down, and cried with a loud voice, Lord, lay not this sin to their charge. And when he had said this, he fell asleep" (Acts 7:55,60).

God even rewarded Stephen at the losing of his life. Jesus rose and stood at the right hand of the Father to welcome Stephen's entry into the glory.

The Apostle Paul experienced loss of position, prestige and influence. Let him tell the story in his own words: "Circumcised the eighth day, of the stock of Israel, of the tribe of Benjamin, an Hebrew of the Hebrews; as touching the law, a Pharisee; Concerning zeal, persecuting the church; touching the righteousness which is in the law, blameless. But what things were gain to me, those I counted loss for Christ. Yea doubtless, and I count all things but loss for the excellency of the knowledge of Christ Jesus my Lord: for Whom I have suffered the loss of all things, and do count them but dung, that I may win Christ," (Philippians 3:5-8).

You must see treasures beyond your losses.

The Double Portion Blessing Of God Can Follow Every Major Loss. It happened to Job when he lost his children, his flocks and herds, and his position of credibility and popularity. "And the Lord turned the captivity of Job, when he prayed for his friends: also the Lord gave Job twice as much as he had before. Then came there unto him all his brethren, and all his sisters, and all they that had been of his acquaintance before, and did eat bread with him in his house: and they bemoaned him, and comforted him over all the evil that the Lord had brought upon him: every man also gave him a piece of money, and every one an earring of gold. So the Lord blessed the latter end of Job more than his beginning: for he had fourteen thousand sheep, and six thousand camels, and a thousand yoke of oxen, and a thousand she asses. He had also seven sons and three daughters. And he called the name of the first, Jemima; and the name of the second, Kezia; and the name of the third, Kerenhappuch. And in all the land were no women found *so* fair as the daughters of Job: and their father gave them inheritance among their brethren. After this lived Job an hundred and forty years, and saw his sons, and his sons' sons, even four generations. So Job died, being old and full of days" (Job 42:10-17).

Remember: *Obedience To Your Assignment May Create A Temporary Season Of Loss.*

⹂ 53 ⹂

YOUR ASSIGNMENT MAY FIRST APPEAR TO BE UNDESIRABLE AND EVEN REPULSIVE.

Uncommon Gifts Can Come In Unattractive Packaging.
Divinity differs from humanity.
Man sees the immediate.
God sees the *eventuality*.
"...for the Lord seeth not as man seeth; for man looketh on the outward appearance, but the Lord looketh on the heart" (1 Samuel 16:7).

Calvary was not a desirable Assignment to Jesus. Consider Jesus. He was pure, yet called to minister to the impure. He was holy, yet called to live around the unholy. He was brilliant, yet assigned to the ignorant. He was perfect, yet assigned to live with the imperfect.

Now, observe His cry as He enters the crucial part of his entire Assignment on earth, the crucifixion. He is in the Garden of Gethsemane. His disciples are asleep. It seems that God Himself has turned His back on Him, the Son. He weeps desperately, "O My Father, if it be possible, let this cup pass from Me: nevertheless not as I will, but as Thou wilt" (Matthew 26:39).

Titus had a repulsive Assignment. Paul writes to him to reassure him. He knew, "The Cretans are always liars, evil beasts, slow bellies" (Titus 1:12). Then, he explains that that is the very reason why Titus was chosen and assigned to be in Crete! "For this cause left I thee in Crete, that thou shouldest set in order the things that are wanting, and ordain elders in every city, as I had appointed thee:" (Titus 1:5).

Jonah despised his Assignment to Nineveh. "But Jonah rose up to flee unto Tarshish from the presence of the Lord, and went down to Joppa; and he found a ship going to Tarshish:" (Jonah 1:3). Of course, the Bible is also clear about the consequences of his rebellion. He paid for it. "So he paid the fare thereof," (Jonah 1:3). As unappealing and repulsive as parts of your Assignment might appear, nothing is worse than "Seaweed University" in the bottom of the sea. Never forget this.

Jeremiah found his Assignment terribly disheartening. "Oh that I had in the wilderness a lodging place of wayfaring men; that I might leave my people, and go from them! for they be all adulterers, an assembly of treacherous men" (Jeremiah 9:2). He did not even want to stay in the ministry. He despised the low quality of the people to whom he was assigned. He preferred solitude. But, it was his Assignment.

Abraham had painful days in his Assignment. Nothing could be more devastating than an instruction he received from the Lord. "And he said, Take now thy son, thine only *son* Isaac, whom thou lovest, and get thee into the land of Moriah; and offer him there for a burnt offering upon one of the mountains which I will tell thee of" (Genesis 22:2).

This is heartbreaking, repulsive and unexplainable. It is an Assignment that was utterly repulsive. Yet, Abraham knew God. He believed that God always had his best interests at heart.

▶ He obeyed *immediately* and *completely.* He "Who against hope believed in hope, that he might become the father of many nations," (Romans 4:18).

▶ *He refused to disobey. He insisted on believing.* "He staggered not at the promise of God through unbelief; but was strong in faith, giving glory to God;" (Romans 4:20).

▶ He was persuaded concerning *the heart and the ability of God.* "And being fully persuaded that, what He had promised, He was able also to perform" (Romans 4:21).

3 Golden Keys To Remember When Your Assignment Is Heartbreakingly Difficult

1. *When You Doubt Your Instruction, Never Doubt Your Instructor.* "Trust in the Lord with all thine heart; and lean not unto thine own understanding" (Proverbs 3:5).

2.   Remember, *It Is Not The Magnetism Of Those To Whom You Are Assigned, But The Irrefutable And Undeniable, Burning Call Of God Within Your Heart, That Drives You In Your Assignment.* It burned in Jeremiah. "Then I said, I will not make mention of Him, nor speak any more in His name. But His Word was in mine heart as a burning fire shut up in my bones, and I was weary with forbearing, and I could not stay" (Jeremiah 20:9).

3.   *Always Remember That Nothing Is Ever As Bad As It First Appears.* Nothing. Beyond the crucifixion is a resurrection.

"They that sow in tears shall reap in joy. He that goeth forth and weepeth, bearing precious seed, shall doubtless come again with rejoicing, bringing His sheaves with Him" (Psalm 126:5,6).

"Weeping may endure for a night, but joy cometh in the morning" (Psalm 30:5).

▶ Beyond the lion's den is a promotion.

▶ Beyond tears, there is laughter.

Remember: *Your Assignment May First Appear To Be Undesirable And Even Repulsive.*

Champions Do Things
They Hate
To Create Something Else
They Love.

-MIKE MURDOCK

⇜ 54 ⇝

YOUR ASSIGNMENT MAY REQUIRE PERIODIC SEPARATION FROM THOSE YOU LOVE.

Solitude Is Often Necessary For Impartation.
It is normal to love the atmosphere of friends. Connection is essential for multiplication. It takes two to become more. "Two *are* better than one;" (Ecclesiastes 4:9). *But, your Assignment will have many moments of withdrawing from others.*

Jesus withdrew Himself from the multitudes. "But so much the more went there a fame abroad of Him: and great multitudes came together to hear, and to be healed by Him of their infirmities. And He withdrew Himself into the wilderness, and prayed" (Luke 5:15,16).

"Now when Jesus saw great multitudes about Him, He gave commandment to depart unto the other side" (Matthew 8:18).

Jesus taught His followers to come apart from others for times of restoration. And He said unto them, "Come ye yourselves apart into a desert place, and rest a while: for there were many coming and going, and they had no leisure so much as to eat. And they departed into a desert place by ship privately" (Mark 6:31,32).

Jesus withdrew from the pressure of people, knowing that ministry is emptying. Restoring others requires emptying yourself. When others reach, they draw something out of you. Jesus experienced this with the woman who had an issue of blood for twelve years. "For she said, If I may touch but His clothes, I shall be whole" (Mark 5:28). It did happen. But Jesus felt something leave Him. "And Jesus, immediately knowing in Himself that virtue had gone out of Him, turned Him about in the press, and said, Who touched My clothes?" (Mark 5:30).

▶ Sometimes, you must withdraw from the *pressure* of

people.

▶ Sometimes, you must withdraw from the *pleasure* of people.

So, God will often speak to you to have moments away from those you love.

It will restore you and strengthen you.

It will also enable you to hear His voice without the stain and distortion of human logic and opinions.

Sometimes, your Assignment will cost you wonderful moments of conversation and relaxation times. It is the opposite of rest times. It will demand *all* of you. It will require your total absorption and concentration.

I am sitting in my Wisdom Room dictating this to you. There are books wall-to-wall and ceiling-to-floor. I absolutely love books. I love biographies and success books. And I love collecting new ones monthly.

Next to this room is the most important room in my home, The Secret Place. It is a small but power-filled room dedicated to the Holy Spirit. He dramatically affected my life on July 13, 1994, and I have been a different man since that day. My yard is large, but it has speakers on the trees that play Holy Spirit music continuously.

Yet, I spend my life traveling thousands of miles every month *away from here.* I spend most of my life sleeping in strange little bedrooms in strange hotels in strange cities. I sit in a tiny cramped airplane seat for hours, with thoughts of being in my recliner in my Wisdom Room, reading!

I long to stay home. Traveling is not exciting to me any more. I have done it for more than thirty years. Then, why do I stay in cramped little hotel quarters, rushing from airport to airport just to speak for a few minutes to audiences across this globe?

It is The Assignment.

Occasionally, I feel sorry for myself. Sometimes, I envy those who wake up in the same bed every morning, eating breakfast at the same table, and seeing faithful and loyal friends every day of their lives. Sometimes, I have to remind myself that, "This world is not my home, I am just passing through. I am a pilgrim. I am a wayfarer." It is not always easy to walk away from pleasurable surroundings.

I love my staff. It has taken me thirty years to have the team of champions that surround me daily. I admire them. I respect them. They are my family. Yet, I rarely get to spend long hours and days with them. The Assignment is my obsession.

Last night, I had an intense desire to lean back and watch some videos. I was tired. I just had an incredible week of meetings. God had moved. People were radically touched and restored. I really did not want to work late last night at all. But, I looked at the letters of partners and those who had written me.

They deserved an answer. Like Jesus, "...when He saw the multitudes, He was moved with compassion on them, because they fainted, and were scattered abroad, as sheep having no shepherd" (Matthew 9:36).

Compassion is a force. A powerful force. It is something I cannot explain. When I turned 50 years old I spoke on the subject, "Fifty years: My Memories, Mistakes and Miracles." I told my family of partners, and friends that I could not explain compassion. When you care about people, you are driven to minister to them. It is something overpowering, unexplainable and unavoidable when you get in His presence.

Satan often exploits this compassion to drive us into achievements that God never instructed. I am very aware that some of our drive and energy can become ambition, uncontrolled and undirected by the Holy Spirit. This has happened in thousands of lives. However, it cannot be denied either that His calling can so dominate your life that you forfeit moments of pleasure and things that you would love to be doing.

Why do we withdraw from pleasurable moments from those we love? *The Harvest beckons.* "Then saith He unto His disciples, The harvest truly *is* plenteous, but the labourers are few; Pray ye therefore the Lord of the harvest, that He will send forth labourers into His harvest" (Matthew 9:37,38).

One of the greatest evangelists in history told me of his deep love for the game of golf.

"How often do you go golfing?"

"Every chance I get," he answered.

"Do you go daily?" I asked.

"I would if I had the time," was his strong reply. But, he had an Assignment. He trains thousands of people for the ministry every year.

Something matters far more than our pleasure.

Tomorrow will last longer than today.

▶ *Champions Are Willing To Do Things They Hate To Create Something They Love.*

▶ *Champions Make Decisions That Create Their Desired Future While Losers Make The Decisions That Create Their Desired Present.*

There is a costly season for *sowing* your life into *others*. "And Jesus saith unto him, The foxes have holes, and the birds of the air have nests; but the Son of man hath not where to lay His head" (Matthew 8:20).

There is a compensation season for *reaping* from the One Who gave you your Assignment. "And let us not be weary in well doing: for in due season we shall reap, if we faint not" (Galatians 6:9).

Peter experienced aloneness. He must have felt the loneliness of withdrawing from those he loved. He missed the vibrant and exciting atmosphere of the fishing boats at times. "Then Peter began to say unto Him, Lo, we have left all, and have followed Thee" (Mark 10:28).

Jesus guaranteed reward on the other side of separation. He made a powerful, incredible and marvelous response. I cannot say it any better than our precious Lord said it that day: "And Jesus answered and said, Verily I say unto you, There is no man that hath left house, or brethren, or sisters, or father, or mother, or wife, or children, or lands, for My sake, and the gospel's, But he shall receive an hundredfold now in this time, houses, and brethren, and sisters, and mothers, and children, and lands, with persecutions; and in the world to come eternal life" (Mark 10:29,30).

You will never regret pursuing your Assignment.

But, it is true. Remember: *Your Assignment May Require Periodic Separation From Those You Love.*

❧ 55 ❧

YOUR ASSIGNMENT MAY REQUIRE YOU TO WALK AWAY FROM SOMETHING IMPORTANT TO YOU.

➤➤●◆◄◄

Comfort Is Addictive.

Every tiny action in your life is always a step away from perceived *pain* or a step toward anticipated *gain*. It is normal to pursue increase, comfort and promotion. It is normal to become attached to the things that really matter to us, such as our home, family or a cherished possession.

When God births your Assignment, it often requires you to walk away from something you want very much; a treasured friendship, a cherished possession or even a deeply rooted belief system and philosophy.

You may be required to walk away from a proven source of income. Peter did. "And Jesus answered and said, Verily I say unto you, There is no man that hath left house, or brethren, or sisters, or father, or mother, or wife, or children, or lands, for My sake, and the gospel's, But he shall receive an hundredfold now in this time, houses, and brethren, and sisters, and mothers, and children, and lands, with persecutions; and in the world to come eternal life" (Mark 10:29,30).

James and John walked away from their fishing business. "And going on from thence, He saw other two brethren, James the son of Zebedee, and John his brother, in a ship with Zebedee their father, mending their nets; and He called them. And they immediately left the ship and their father, and followed Him" (Matthew 4:21,22).

You may be required to leave the comfort of your home, family and relatives. Abraham did. "Now the Lord had said unto Abram, Get thee out of thy country, and from thy kindred, and from thy father's house, unto a land that I will shew thee:" (Genesis 12:1).

Ruth left her home country. "And Ruth said, Intreat me not to leave thee, or to return from following after thee: for whither thou goest, I will go; and where thou lodgest, I will lodge: thy people shall be my people, and thy God my God: Where thou diest, will I die, and there will I be buried: the Lord do so to me, and more also, if ought but death part thee and me" (Ruth 1:16,17).

I understand this kind of commitment. It happens in my own life every single week. I love my Schools of the Holy Spirit hosted each month in some of the top cities of America. I love talking to pastor friends as I minister in their churches. Ministering and teaching in conferences, seminars and crusades is a very pleasurable and wonderful Assignment on earth. However, I love my home. When I am at home, I never want to leave. In fact, I have done without meals just to avoid driving out of the driveway! Though a major mall is fifteen minutes from my house, I would rather stay home and eat a sandwich than drive fifteen minutes to a major restaurant.

I have traveled widely, including trips to 38 nations of the world. I have seen the pyramids, the catacombs and Mt. Kilimanjaro. I have spent many months in Africa, Switzerland, Germany, Russia, India, France and England. The list goes on. But, I would rather be at home reading and seeking the face of God in The *Secret Place.*

Your Assignment may require you to release something important to you.

Concentrate on the Rewards of Obedience.

Now, the rewards are obvious, inevitable and consistent. And, that is really how God keeps motivating me to obey Him. "If ye be willing and obedient, ye shall eat the good of the land:" (Isaiah 1:19).

Remain aware of the consequences of missing the will of God. "But if ye refuse and rebel, ye shall be devoured with the sword: for the mouth of the Lord hath spoken it" (Isaiah 1:20).

I have a healthy fear of God. It was birthed and nurtured from my childhood years. My mother constantly reminded me that "The fear of the Lord is the beginning of wisdom:" (Proverbs 9:10). I knew the rewards of Wisdom! "For by Me thy days shall be multiplied, and the years of thy life shall be increased" (Proverbs 9:11). "Riches and honour are with Me; yea, durable riches and righteousness. My fruit is better than gold, yea, than fine gold; and My revenue than choice silver...That I may cause those that love Me to inherit substance; and I will fill their treasures" (Proverbs 8:18,19,21).

The incentives are obvious and proven. So, I am willing to walk away from something important to me in order to pursue something which benefits me *more*.

God sometimes uses an experience to break your addiction to a possession, a comfort zone or even a relationship.

I remember a deeply cherished earthly possession of many years ago, a beautiful, rare gold watch. I bought it in Lausanne, Switzerland. I never saw another one like it. There were only two made like it in the world. It had a beautiful fifty carat quartz stone on top. Several friends wanted to purchase it from me. It was gorgeous. It was my point of significance from those around me!

One morning, during a season of great adversity, I rushed out the door to take some clothes to the cleaners. Because I was in a rush, I simply placed my watch on top of the shirts in my lap as I drove to the cleaners. I intended to put it on as I was driving. Something distracted me and when I arrived at the cleaners, it was still on the pile of shirts.

I rushed inside and left my clothes, and rushed on to my office. Suddenly, it dawned on me that I was not wearing my watch. I telephoned the cleaners and returned to look for it. They denied that the watch was in the cleaning. Perhaps, it fell off the shirt load as I stepped out of the car. I will never know. I was heartbroken.

Also, because of the turmoil of the court trials I was experiencing, I had neglected to keep the insurance coverage current! I could never collect on it. I felt so dead and sick inside. As I walked through my office praying quietly in the Holy Spirit, I could not believe that I had lost my most valued material possession. I valued it above my home, my car and everything else. Suddenly, the Holy Spirit spoke a simple sentence to me. "Hold loosely to the things of this world."

I have never forgotten that sentence to this day.

I do not have a thing that did not come from the Lord anyhow.

Everything I have was *given* to me.

Everything I possess is something I have *received from Another.*

Whatever you give up in the pursuit of your Assignment, I promise you that God will repay you one hundred times over. You have *His* Word on it. "And Jesus answered and said, Verily I say unto you, There is no man that hath left house, or brethren, or sisters, or father, or mother, or wife, or children, or lands, for my sake, and the gospel's, But he shall receive an hundredfold now in this time, houses, and brethren, and sisters, and mothers, and children, and lands, with persecutions; and in the world to come eternal life" (Mark 10:29,30).

It is in the Eternal Contract of the Kingdom.

I received a disturbing telephone call several years ago. One of my college buddies had a crisis in his marriage. He felt impressed of God to accept a pastorate. His wife refused to move.

"Mike, I really love my wife and I want peace in my marriage. She refuses to accept the calling of God to this new church. What should I do?"

"I would embrace it in two ways: First, I would permit her to be a corrective influence. God gave her to you for a reason. She is the gift of God to your life. She brings balance. Perhaps it is not the will of God for you to go to the church. Get into The Secret Place. Ask the Lord if He is using her as a corrective measure to help you stay on course. You may have a vision produced by your imagination. She may have the balance and practicality of building where you are."

I continued, "Secondly, if you go to The Secret Place and receive affirmation from the Holy Spirit that you indeed are in the will of God, embrace the challenge of teaching and mentoring her to *hear the voice of God.* Show her the rewards of obedience. Begin to nurture in her the importance of both of you following the Lord. Remind her how precious and special she is to your life. She is like the body of Christ is to Jesus. Emphasize your need for her to stand by your side."

He agreed. Some days later, the phone rang again. She was adamant. She refused to move or even consider discussion. After encouraging him to go to a marriage counselor, I entered into a prayer of agreement with him on the telephone that he would have the courage to do the will of God *regardless of the cost.*

According to a recent conversation, the family has been fragmented. He chose to stay instead of accepting the church God had spoken to him about. He is miserable and so is the entire family. He failed the test of leadership—*the willingness to do the will of God alone if necessary.*

I am persuaded your *family is important.*

I am persuaded your *mate is important.*

I am persuaded your *marriage is important.*

I am more persuaded that doing *the will of God* is the most important decision of your lifetime.

Your Assignment is more important than any other relationship in your life. It is that invisible and overpowering calling that causes an evangelist to travel day after day, to strange airports and hotels and even away from the family who may refuse to follow him.

It is what makes a great missionary travel all over East Africa and not see his own children for many months. He loves the United States. He enjoys the pleasure of nice hotels. He cherishes the laughter of his grandchildren. But, his Assignment cannot be changed by him or anybody else. He knows it.

The price is great.

But, the peace is worth it.

Obviously, there are carnal and manipulative people who would twist the Scriptures to accommodate their own lust of the flesh. They leave families, children, husbands and wives and do it "in the name of the Lord." This is ridiculous and deceptive. God will never destroy your marriage or your home. It is not the will of God. He is a God who heals, restores and mends. The emphasis I place here is total obedience to the calling of God, *whatever the cost.*

Remember: *Your Assignment May Require You To Walk Away From Something Important To You.*

What You Can Walk Away From
You Have Mastered-
What You Cannot Walk Away From
Has Mastered You.

-MIKE MURDOCK

≈ 56 ≈

WHAT YOU ARE WILLING TO WALK AWAY FROM DETERMINES WHAT GOD WILL BRING TO YOU.

Your Future Is Much Greater Than Your Present.

You simply must be willing to walk away from your present. God has plans. He has bigger plans than your imagination could ever create for a lifetime.

If you are willing to walk away from something important to you, God will compensate you over and over again.

If you fail to walk away, the consequences and the disasters are also inevitable.

3 Tragic Examples Of Those Who Refused To Walk Away

Samson refused to walk away from Delilah. He became a joke and a sport to the Philistines. His eyes were gouged out. His days of championship were over.

Judas refused to walk away from thirty pieces of silver. He committed suicide. His name will never be recorded in the Heroes' Hall of Faith.

Demas would not walk away from the magnetism of the world. He became a mere footnote in the writings of Paul. "For Demas hath forsaken me, having loved this present world, and is departed" (2 Timothy 4:10).

3 Champions Who Were Willing To Walk Away

Moses was willing to walk away from the palace of Pharaoh. He esteemed the reproach of Christ to be greater than the treasures of Egypt. The favor of God surrounded him and hundreds of years after his death, he is mentioned as one of the Heroes of Faith in Hebrews 11. "By faith Moses, when he was come to years, refused to be called the son of Pharaoh's daughter; Choosing rather to suffer affliction with the people of God, than to enjoy the pleasures of sin for a season; Esteeming the reproach of Christ greater riches than the treasures in Egypt: for he had respect unto the recompense of the reward. By faith he forsook Egypt, not fearing the wrath of the king: for he endured, as seeing Him who is invisible" (Hebrews 11:24-27).

Joseph was willing to walk away from the temptation of Potiphar's wife. God gave him the throne. He became Prime Minister and one of the most revered men of God in the entire Bible.

Ruth was willing to walk away from Moab. She met a remarkable, wealthy and godly man named Boaz. They produced a son, Obed, who produced Jesse. Jesse, the father of David and grandfather of Solomon, ushered in the lineage of Jesus of Nazareth.

What You Are Willing To Walk Away From Determines Who God Will Bring Into Your Life As Well.

Are you single? I have been single for many years. In my early years of singleness, loneliness was often overpowering. I became militant, argumentative and agitated with God. I wanted to hold on to wrong relationships that helped to distract me from the pain and emptiness of aloneness. But, God reminded me of this powerful principle: *What You Are Willing To Walk Away From Determines What He Will Bring To You.*

5 Rules For Relationships

1. Never Stay *Where* You Have Not Been Assigned.
2. Never Stay Around *Someone* Who Is Not Assigned To You.
3. Never Stay Where You Are Not *Celebrated*.
4. Never Stay In A Relationship That Feeds Your *Weakness,* Instead Of Your Strength.
5. Never Stay In A Relationship That *Keeps* You In Your *Present,* Instead Of *Moving* You Toward Your *Future*.

It is often difficult to end a comfortable relationship. It is difficult to walk away from a relationship that eases the loneliness, the inner vacuum that distracts you from your solitary times. But often, when God gives you an Assignment, He will require you to give up a relationship that really matters to you.

That is why Jesus hastened to reassure Peter that any losses would be *recognized and restored* if total obedience occurred. "Then Peter began to say unto Him, Lo, we have left all, and have followed Thee. And Jesus answered and said, Verily I say unto you, There is no man that hath left house, or brethren, or sisters, or father, or mother, or wife, or children, or lands, for My sake, and the gospel's, But he shall receive an hundredfold now in this time, houses, and brethren, and sisters, and mothers, and children, and lands, with persecutions; and in the world to come eternal life" (Mark 10:28-30).

God may require you to temporarily walk away from financial security. The widow of Zarephath had to walk away from her last meal. She was starving. The famine was everywhere. Elijah showed up at her door with a request. "And Elijah said unto her, Fear not; go and do as thou hast said: but make me thereof a little cake first, and bring it unto me, and after make for thee and for thy son" (1 Kings 17:13).

What a rare and difficult decision she was forced to make! Her son was dying. He was emaciated, weakened and almost dead. It was to be their last meal together. A man of God instructed her to *walk away* from her own provision, her last meal on earth. People sometimes criticize ministers who ask for donations to their vision. They sneer and make snide remarks about a man of God who strongly urges them to sow their Seed into the soil of lost souls. Television commentators often target ministers who emphasize finances in any way. Yet, Elijah instructed a woman to *walk away* from her Seed, *her last meal.*

She obeyed.

Her *future* was more important than her *present.*

Her *Seed* was more important than her *meal.*

His *word* was more important than her *pain.*

The prophet explained the Principle of Increase: "For thus saith the Lord God of Israel, The barrel of meal shall not waste, neither shall the cruse of oil fail, until the day that the Lord sendeth rain upon the earth. And she went and did according to the saying of Elijah: and she, and he, and her house, did eat many days. And the barrel of meal wasted not, neither did the cruse of oil fail, according to the word of the Lord, which he spake by Elijah" (1 Kings 17:14-16).

Here is her incentive for obedience: *provision.*

What You Are Willing To Walk Away From Determines What God Will Bring To You.

My $8,500 Miracle

A remarkable experience happened in my life several years ago.

I had just received a royalty check for more than $8,500 from my song writing. I was ecstatic. I had just completed three crusades in Poland, East Africa and Brazil. I had arrived home, and went straight to preach for a minister friend of mine, Rod Parsley in Columbus, Ohio. At the conclusion of the service, I turned the service to Pastor Parsley to receive an offering for my ministry. Just as I was about to hand the microphone to him, the Holy Spirit instructed me to receive a special offering for the pastor instead of my own ministry. I have always been swift to obey the Lord, so I proceeded.

Suddenly, while I was explaining to the people that there would be no offering received for me at all, we would give one to the pastor and his wife instead, the Holy Spirit spoke. It was not a command. It was not really an instruction. It was more like a suggestion. It seemed like an *invitation to an investment.* I had never had such an experience before.

"How would you like to explore and experiment with what I could do with your $8,500?"

I froze. This $8,500 was my *Harvest.* I was thrilled. I had great plans how to spend it. It was going to be *fun* money. He spoke again in the form of a question.

"How would you like to *explore and experiment* with what I could do with your $8,500?"

I knew His voice. I was in His presence. I have spent many years preaching this gospel around the world. He was giving me an opportunity to prove His power, His love and His creativity in my life. I thought for several minutes. Actually, I thought for about 45 minutes. What could I do with $8,500? *That was a lot of money!* But, I kept thinking. I could buy a small car, fly to Europe and live for about thirty days or I could put a down payment on a small rent house somewhere.

I thought a second time. *What could He do with my $8,500?* I remembered the five loaves and two fishes of the little boy. Jesus used them to feed the multitude. As long as the little boy was holding the five loaves and two fishes, it remained just five loaves and two fishes. It dawned on me...

Nothing Multiplies Until It Is In The Hands Of Jesus. It is always His touch that brings the multiplication.

If I *kept* the $8,500, $8,500 is the *most* it would ever be.

If I *sowed* the $8,500, $8,500 is the *least* it would ever be.

Then, I asked myself another question. Is $8,500 all I will ever need *the rest of my life*? Is that enough money to do my entire future vision and goals and dreams? Of course not. I had to realize it myself. One car alone would cost much more than $8,500. A new home would cost many times more than that amount. Something within me rose up strongly to believe God. I chose to believe that He wanted to *bless* me.

▶ I chose to believe my future could be *unlike my present*.
▶ I chose to *honor* the inner whisperings of the Holy Spirit.
▶ I chose to *use my faith* at one of the highest levels in my lifetime.

I planted the entire $8,500 as a Seed of Faith.

When I walked into my hotel room that night, I plummeted into an unexplainable depression. I could hardly speak for seven days. Satan worked on my mind. He continuously sneered and laughed and said to me, "That was not the Holy Spirit at all. That was your imagination that told you to plant the $8,500. It was not God. You will never see any results to this Seed. You have just lost $8,500."

I felt sick inside. I really believed him. I felt stupid. I felt ignorant. I felt like I had been taken in by my own weakness and sowed a Seed that was unnecessary in response to an imagination of my own mind.

About seven days later, I cried out to God in my Secret Place. "I sowed this Seed of $8,500 in an attempt to obey you. If I missed Your will, I am sorry, but I did it in an attempt to please You."

He spoke only one sentence back to my heart but I have never forgotten that sentence: "Anything you do in an attempt to please Me, will not go unrewarded."

Anything You Do In An Attempt To Please God Will Not Go Unrewarded.

Six weeks later, I was staying at the Hyatt Regency Hotel in Houston, Texas. I arose at 5:30 a.m. for my prayer time. At 7:15 a.m., the Holy Spirit suddenly gave me an idea. It was to take 2,000 Scriptures and place them in categories for businessmen. I decided to call it, "The Businessman's Topical Bible." It would make it possible for any Christian businessman to find a Scripture within ten seconds concerning any difficult season he was experiencing in business.

Then, I saw a photograph in my heart of "The Mother's Topical Bible." It would help mothers to find Scriptures by categories, depending on the difficulty they were going through with their husbands or children. The same picture came to me for "The Father's Topical Bible." Then, I saw another one in my heart— "The Teenager's Topical Bible."

I telephoned a publisher. They agreed to pay me a royalty from each Bible printed. They promised to place the Bibles in 1,300 bookstores across the United States on a regular basis. They would give me a royalty percentage of every one that sold for the remaining of the contract as long as I wanted it.

God has since blessed those Topical Bibles beyond my imagination. To date, over 2 million have been sold!

In fact, when a major Christian booksellers' association chose the top one hundred reference books in the United States, five of the first twenty were my topical Bibles! I was able to buy my mother and father cars, renovate their home and help put young preachers through Bible college. Every ninety days, I still receive a royalty check.

I was willing to walk away from the $8,500.

God has rewarded me many, many times over.

Your Willingness To Walk Away From Your Present Is Your Greatest Qualification For Your Future.

I shared this in Florida some months ago. A woman approached me and asked me to anoint her special Seed for $8,500. She had heard me say that God had given me a *lifetime income from a one-time Seed.* She wanted to experience the same miracle by planting a Lifetime Blessing Seed of $8,500.

I agreed to covenant with her that God would do for her exactly what He had done for me. Within months, she settled a lawsuit. Her reward? More than $400,000.

What You Are Willing To Walk Away From Determines What God Will Bring To You.

God may be speaking to you this very moment. He may be talking to you about planting a significant and powerful Seed into His work. It keeps arising in your mind. It stays in your heart. Yet, your own bills and needs appear overpowering. You are facing a mountain of debt. You are hesitant, even fearful. Let me encourage you today to embrace the words of God to you.

God will never lie to you. "God is not a man, that He should lie; neither the son of man, that He should repent: hath He said, and shall He not do it? or hath He spoken, and shall He not make it good?" (Numbers 23:19).

Remember: *What You Are Willing To Walk Away From Determines What God Will Bring To You.*

RECOMMENDED BOOKS AND TAPES

B-15   Seeds Of Wisdom On Miracles (32 pages/$3)
B-82   31 Reasons People Do Not Receive Their Financial
         Harvest (229 pages/$12)
TSB-82   31 Reasons People Do Not Receive Their Financial
         Harvest (6 tapes/$30)
B-104   7 Keys To 1000 Times More (124 pages/$10)
B-151   The Craziest Instruction God Ever Gave Me (144 pages/$10)

Broken People
Become Masters
At Mending.

-MIKE MURDOCK

～ 57 ～

IT IS POSSIBLE TO BE RESTORED AFTER YOU HAVE MADE A MAJOR MISTAKE IN YOUR ASSIGNMENT.

━━━━◆◆◆◆━━━━

Mistakes Are Gates.

A mistake is not a conclusion. A mistake is an entry into another season.

14 Facts You Should Know About Your Mistakes

1. *Recognize That God Anticipates Your Mistakes.* "For He knoweth our frame; He remembereth that we are dust...But the mercy of the Lord is from everlasting to everlasting upon them that fear Him, and His righteousness unto children's children;" (Psalm 103:14,17).

2. *When You Make A Mistake, Have An Immediate Conference With God.* "Come now, and let us reason together, saith the Lord: though your sins be as scarlet, they shall be as white as snow; though they be red like crimson, they shall be as wool" (Isaiah 1:18).

3. *Remember, No Mistake Is Too Big To Be Forgiven.* Listen to Paul. "This *is* a faithful saying, and worthy of all acceptation, that Christ Jesus came into the world to save sinners; of whom I am chief. Howbeit for this cause I obtained mercy, that in me first Jesus Christ might shew forth all longsuffering, for a pattern to them which should hereafter believe on Him to life everlasting" (1 Timothy 1:15,16).

4. *Believe That Mistakes Will Never Erase The Love Of Christ Toward You.* "Who shall separate us from the love of Christ? shall

tribulation, or distress, or persecution, or famine, or nakedness, or peril, or sword? As it is written, For Thy sake we are killed all the day long; we are accounted as sheep for the slaughter. Nay, in all these things we are more than conquerors through Him that loved us. For I am persuaded, that neither death, nor life, nor angels, nor principalities, nor powers, nor things present, nor things to come, Nor height, nor depth, nor any other creature, shall be able to separate us from the love of God, which is in Christ Jesus our Lord" (Romans 8:35-39).

5. *Look For The Plans Of God On The Other Side Of Your Mistakes.* Why does He endure and show longsuffering to us? "And that He might make known the riches of His glory on the vessels of mercy," (Romans 9:23).

6. *Expect Your Tragedies To Become Your Trophies.* David is an eternal Trophy on display in the Museum of Miracles. Carefully listen to his heart's cry after adultery with Bathsheba and having her husband, Uriah, murdered on the field of battle. "Wash me throughly from mine iniquity, and cleanse me from my sin. For I acknowledge my transgressions: and my sin is ever before me...Purge me with hyssop, and I shall be clean: wash me, and I shall be whiter than snow. Make me to hear joy and gladness; that the bones which Thou hast broken may rejoice. Hide Thy face from my sins, and blot out all mine iniquities. Create in me a clean heart, O God; and renew a right spirit within me. Cast me not away from Thy presence; and take not Thy Holy Spirit from me. Restore unto me the joy of thy salvation; and uphold me with Thy free spirit" (Psalm 51:2,3,7-12).

7. *Hate The Mistake Enough To Repent And Turn From It.* "But shewed first unto them of Damascus, and at Jerusalem, and throughout all the coasts of Judaea, and then to the Gentiles, that they should repent and turn to God, and do works meet for repentance" (Acts 26:20).

8. *Acknowledge Your Transgression And Ask For Restoration.* "Ask, and it shall be given you; seek, and ye shall find; knock, and it shall be opened unto you: For every one that asketh receiveth; and he that seeketh findeth; and to him that knocketh it shall be opened" (Matthew 7:7,8).

9. *Recognize That Your Heavenly Father Is The Only One Who Can Make You Clean Again.* Your personal works, resolutions

and vows will not restore you. "For by grace are ye saved through faith; and that not of yourselves: it is the gift of God: Not of works, lest any man should boast" (Ephesians 2:8,9). Any damaged product must be returned to the manufacturer for repairs.

10. *Confess Mistakes To Those In Spiritual Authority Over Your Life Who Can Pray A Prayer Of Deliverance.* "Confess your faults one to another, and pray one for another, that ye may be healed. The effectual fervent prayer of a righteous man availeth much" (James 5:16).

11. *Pursue And Permit Restoration By Those Who Love You.* "Brethren, if a man be overtaken in a fault, ye which are spiritual, restore such an one in the spirit of meekness; considering thyself, lest thou also be tempted" (Galatians 6:1).

12. *Restore Anything You Have Wrongly Taken From Another.* Zacchaeus understood this principle. "And Zacchaeus stood, and said unto the Lord; Behold, Lord, the half of my goods I give to the poor; and if I have taken any thing from any man by false accusation, I restore him fourfold" (Luke 19:8).

13. *Focus On Your Future Instead Of Your Failure.* "Remember ye not the former things, neither consider the things of old. Behold, I will do a new thing: now it shall spring forth; shall ye not know it? I will even make a way in the wilderness, and rivers in the desert" (Isaiah 43:18,19).

14. *Teach Others The Laws Of Restoration.* David declared that when God restored him, he would teach others the laws of restoration. "Then will I teach transgressors thy ways; and sinners shall be converted unto Thee" (Psalm 51:13).

Would you take a moment to pray this brief prayer with me today? Will you pray this sincerely from the depths of your heart?

"Heavenly Father,

I know I have sinned.

I hate the mistakes in my life.

Somehow, You have given me another day to pursue You and begin changes.

I cannot do it alone.

You alone can change my heart, my desires and my destiny.

I choose to believe that Your *mercy* is more powerful than my *mistakes*.

Your *love* is more powerful than my *losses*.

Your *power* is stronger than my *pain*.

Your *Wisdom* can mend my weakness.

You are my God.

I am Your child.

Begin the changes in me today.

Forgive me of every sin: as I submit totally to Your authority and life today.

I believe that Your blood cleanses and purifies every stain on my conscience, my memories and my life.

From this moment forward, I will follow You as Savior, Lord and Master of my life.

In Jesus' name, confirm Your presence by Your instant peace and overwhelming joy this very moment. Amen and Amen."

Now, rise up again! And remember, permit those closest to you to receive *that same mercy.*

Broken People Become Masters At Mending.

Begin to mend those around you this very day.

Remember: *It Is Possible To Be Restored After You Have Made A Major Mistake In Your Assignment.*

⁓ 58 ⁓

THE BIBLE REVEALS THE RECOVERY SYSTEM FOR ANYONE WHO FAILS IN THEIR ASSIGNMENT.

Everybody Falls.

Champions get back up.

Study the life of Peter. It is always wise to attend the Personal Workshop of Peter, when he teaches on "The Laws of Restoration." He tasted personal failure. When he denied the Lord three times, the sudden realization of his weakness was overwhelming. "And he went out, and wept bitterly" (Matthew 26:75). Nobody will ever know the emotional havoc Peter experienced in his heart and soul. It is quite possible that he considered suicide like Judas. It is likely that he felt unwanted, undesirable and unnecessary.

But, somewhere in his relationship with Jesus, he caught a glimpse of mercy. *He had studied love with the Master of Love.* He had studied The Laws of Restoration from the One Who restored thousands in a moment. He had watched Jesus look up into a tree, then have supper with a deceptive tax collector. He had memories of the demon possessed being set free by their deliverer.

Oh, you and I serve a second-chance God! I wrote a wonderful song several years ago called, "He's Done it Once, He's Done it Twice and He Can Do it Again."

♪♪ He's done it once.
He's done it twice.
And, He can do it again.

He's done it once. ♪

♪ He's done it twice.
♪ And, He can do it again.

Every miracle that I need.
Every miracle that I need.

He's done it once.
He's done it twice.
And, He can do it again. ♪

Study the life of Samson.
Samson is remembered on *earth* for Delilah.
Samson is remembered in *Heaven* for his *recovery*.
After his eyes were gouged out, God used him even in his death to kill the enemies of God. "So the dead which he slew in his death were more than they which he slew in his life" (Judges 16:30).
Samson recovered from the shame, the humiliation and embarrassment. In fact, hundreds of years after his death, the writer of the Book of Hebrews included him in the same chapter with Abraham, Moses, Joseph and David.
Study the life of Paul.
Look at this great Apostle. He was a hater, a persecutor of Christians. His name had been Saul. Those who stoned Stephen laid their clothes at his feet. "As for Saul, he made havock of the church, entering into every house, and haling men and women committed them to prison" (Acts 8:3). But, God turned him around.
Is it possible for someone to really change? Ask the Apostle Paul. "And I thank Christ Jesus our Lord, Who hath enabled me, for that He counted me faithful, putting me into the ministry; Who was before a blasphemer, and a persecutor, and injurious: but I obtained mercy, because I did it ignorantly in unbelief. And the grace of our Lord was exceeding abundant with faith and love which is in Christ Jesus" (1 Timothy 1:12-14).
If You Fail During Your Assignment, Pursue The Counsel Of Champions Who Got Back Up.
Remember: *The Bible Reveals The Recovery System For Anyone Who Fails In Their Assignment.*

∼ 59 ∼

GOD IS LOOKING AT SOMETHING IN YOU OTHERS CANNOT SEE.

Something Incredible Is Inside You.

Your Assignment was decided in your mother's womb. "Before I formed thee in the belly I knew thee; and before thou camest forth out of the womb I sanctified thee, and I ordained thee a prophet unto the nations" (Jeremiah 1:5). God knows it. He created you. He has known the invisible purpose for which you were created.

You are not an accident waiting to happen. "I will praise Thee; for I am fearfully and wonderfully made: marvellous are Thy works; and that my soul knoweth right well" (Psalm 139:14).

Everything inside you is known, treasured and intended for full use by your Creator. "My substance was not hid from Thee, when I was made in secret, and curiously wrought in the lowest parts of the earth" (Psalm 139:15).

Your flaws do not necessarily prevent God from using you. They exist to motivate your pursuit of Him. "Thine eyes did see my substance, yet being unperfect; and in Thy book all my members were written, which in continuance were fashioned, when as yet there was none of them" (Psalm 139:16).

Your very existence excites God. "How precious also are Thy thoughts unto me, O God! how great is the sum of them! If I should count them, they are more in number than the sand: when I awake, I am still with Thee" (Psalm 139:17,18).

Picture an author exultant over his book. The book exists. The author created it. He is excited about it, whether anyone else is or not. Imagine a composer, exhilarated over a completed song. He knew its beginning and its ending. Its very presence excites him.

Your very presence energizes God. He saw your beginning and the desired conclusion. "For Thou hast created all things, and for Thy pleasure they are and were created" (Revelation 4:11).

God is looking at something within you *that you have never seen.* "For man looketh on the outward appearance, but the Lord looketh on the heart" (1 Samuel 16:7).

God is looking at something inside you *satan cannot even discern.* "Lest satan should get an advantage of us: for we are ignorant of his devices" (2 Corinthians 2:11).

God is looking at something you contain that *you have not yet discovered.* "For as the heavens are higher than the earth, so are My ways higher than your ways, and My thoughts than your thoughts" (Isaiah 55:9).

God will tell you secrets satan will never hear.

His mercies are not wasted on you. He has big plans. His forgiveness is not futile. You are *becoming* a monument and trophy of His grace. "For we are His workmanship, created in Christ Jesus unto good works," (Ephesians 2:10).

God boasts about you to every demon (see Job 1:8).

You may be looking at your *beginning.*

God is looking at your *end.*

You may be obsessed with your *flaws.*

God is obsessed with your *future.*

You may be focusing on your *enemies.*

God is focusing on your *eventuality.*

God is not *awaiting* your becoming. He is awaiting your *discovery* of it.

So never consult those who have not discovered what is within you. Their focus is different. Their conclusions are inaccurate.

Stay in the presence of the One Who created you. You will always feel confident about yourself when you stay in His presence. He is looking at something in you that is remarkable. He planted it within you while you were yet in your mother's womb.

David understood this. King Saul and his brothers saw brashness; the Holy Spirit saw *boldness.* His brothers saw anger; God saw a sense of *justice.*

Joseph understood this. His brothers saw pride. God saw *thankfulness.* The brothers saw rivalry; God saw a *weapon.*

That is why the opinions and observations of others are not your foundation for greatness. Stop pursuing their conclusions. God is looking at something inside you they *cannot see, refuse* to see and may never see.

The brothers of Jesus did not grasp His *divinity.*

The brothers of Joseph *misinterpreted him.*

The brothers of David saw a mere shepherd boy.

The friends of Job could not discern the satanic scenario *before his crisis.*

Haman could not even discern the nationality of Esther!

Few are ever accurate in their assessment of you. *Few.*

Your flaws are *much less* than they imagine.

Your greatness is far greater than they discern.

The Holy Spirit is the only One Who has accurately assessed your *future,* your *ingredients* and the *willingness* of your heart to become great. That is why He keeps reaching, pursuing and developing you in the midst of every attack and crisis.

He never *gives up* on you.

He never *quits looking at you.*

He never *changes His plans* toward you.

He never quits believing in your future.

He has decided the conclusion and is only awaiting your discovery of it.

Remember this continuously. God is seeing something inside you that keeps Him excited and involved. "Then Samuel took the horn of oil, and anointed him in the midst of his brethren: and the Spirit of the Lord came upon David from that day forward" (1 Samuel 16:13).

Remember: *God Is Looking At Something In You Others Cannot See.*

RECOMMENDED BOOKS AND TAPES

B-56 How To Turn Your Mistakes Into Miracles (32 pages/$3)

Men Decide
  Their Habits...
Their Habits
  Decide Their Future.

-MIKE MURDOCK

☞ 60 ☜

THE SUCCESS OF YOUR ASSIGNMENT IS HIDDEN IN YOUR DAILY ROUTINE.

⟫⟩‒◦‒⟨⟪

Your Daily Habits Create Your Future.

What you do daily determines, what you become permanently. Habit will always take you further than desire.

Creating a perfect day is a vital discovery. Duplicating that kind of day consistently will guarantee uncommon success. Here are seven keys to creating a perfect day in your life.

7 Ingredients Of A Perfect Day

1. *You Must Make Significant And Measurable Movement Toward Good Health.* "What? know ye not that your body is the temple of the Holy Ghost which is in you, which ye have of God, and ye are not your own? For ye are bought with a price: therefore glorify God in your body, and in your spirit, which are God's" (1 Corinthians 6:19,20).

2. *You Must Make Measurable And Significant Movement Toward Order.* Order is the accurate arrangement of things. I have noticed that the smallest effort in drawing up a plan for the day, cleaning out my closet or rearrangement of books in my library, generates joy. The slightest movement toward order generates a measure of pleasure. "But as God hath distributed to every man, as the Lord hath called every one, so let him walk" (1 Corinthians 7:17).

3. *You Must Make Measurable And Significant Movement Toward Uncommon Wisdom.* "Wisdom is the principal thing;" (Proverbs 4:7).

4. *You Must Make Measurable And Significant Movement*

Toward Financial Stability. "Beloved I wish above all things that thou mayest prosper and be in health, even as thy soul prospereth" (3 John 1:2).

5. *You Must Make Measurable And Significant Movement Toward Your Assignment.* "Whatsoever thy hand findeth to do, do it with thy might;" (Ecclesiastes 9:10).

6. *You Must Nurture And Develop Significant Relationships.* You must monitor, motivate and mentor those who are in your Love Circle. "Two are better than one; because they have a good reward for their labour. For if they fall, the one will lift up his fellow: but woe to him that is alone when he falleth; for he hath not another to help him up. And if one prevail against him, two shall withstand him; and a threefold cord is not quickly broken" (Ecclesiastes 4:9,10,12).

7. *You Must Listen Constantly To The Voice Of The Holy Spirit.* He is your lifetime companion. "And I will pray the Father, and He shall give you another Comforter, that He may abide with you for ever; Even the Spirit of truth; Whom the world cannot receive, because it seeth Him not, neither knoweth Him: but ye know Him; for He dwelleth with you, and shall be in you" (John 14:16,17).

Your Assignment is a *daily* miracle.

It is a *daily* event.

You are only responsible for *today.*

When you learn how to obey the voice of the Holy Spirit *hourly,* you will have learned the secret of life.

Remember: *The Success Of Your Assignment Is Hidden In Your Daily Routine.*

≈ 61 ≈

YOUR GREATEST PAIN IS OFTEN CAUSED BY THOSE TO WHOM YOU HAVE BEEN ASSIGNED.

It Is Inevitable.

The servant is not greater than his lord.

Jesus Himself experienced this pain. "O Jerusalem, Jerusalem, thou that killest the prophets, and stonest them which are sent unto thee, how often would I have gathered thy children together, even as a hen gathereth her chickens under her wings, and ye would not!" (Matthew 23:37).

It happened to our precious Savior. And, it will happen to you as well.

Every mother has already experienced this pain. She has known the torment and the toil of a child within her womb for nine months. Then, to watch that child grow up and scream and throw temper tantrums and cry out, "I cannot wait to get away from this house! I hate you!" Every father has known this kind of pain as well.

The comments of neighbors do not necessarily break the heart of parents. It's the comments of the children.

Every pastor knows this pain. He has labored, studied and interceded for his congregation. He has spent hours of counseling and orchestrating the greatest gathering of speakers and others who could minister to his people—only to find out that the family he invested the most time in, has decided to go across town to another church "where they can get their soul fed."

The psalmist knew this pain. "Yea, mine own familiar friend, in whom I trusted, which did eat of my bread, hath lifted up his heel against me" (Psalm 41:9).

Do not be demoralized by the unexpected pain or warfare. It

is normal to every warrior.

It is the Father's secret for feeding your addiction to Him and His presence.

Remember: *Your Greatest Pain Is Often Caused By Those To Whom You Are Assigned.*

～ 62 ～

YOUR ASSIGNMENT WILL REQUIRE THE NATURE, SKILLS AND MENTALITY OF A WARRIOR.

Your Assignment Will Move From Battle To Battle.

Adversity is inevitable. Your enemy observes all progress. God will mentor you in warfare. "He teacheth my hands to war, so that a bow of steel is broken by mine arms" (Psalm 18:34). "Blessed be the Lord my strength, which teacheth my hands to war, and my fingers to fight:" (Psalm 144:1).

18 Qualities Of The Uncommon Warrior

1. *The Uncommon Warrior Only Uses The Weapons That Have Never Failed Him.* He does not use the weapons of others. David used the weapon he was most familiar with—his sling (see 1 Samuel 17:38-40).

2. *The Uncommon Warrior Refuses To Use The Armor And Weaponry Of Others Who Had Failed Before Him.* David did. "And Saul armed David with his armour, and he put an helmet of brass upon his head; also he armed him with a coat of mail. And David girded his sword upon his armour, and he assayed to go; for he had not proved it. And David said unto Saul, I cannot go with these; for I have not proved them. And David put them off him" (1 Samuel 17:38,39).

3. *The Uncommon Warrior Knows He Has Something His Enemy Fears.* David had a willingness to fight. "And David said to Saul, Let no man's heart fail because of him; thy servant will go and fight with this Philistine" (1 Samuel 17:32).

4. *The Uncommon Warrior Knows The True Source Of His Competence And Confidence.* David did. "David said moreover,

The Lord that delivered me out of the paw of the lion, and out of the paw of the bear, He will deliver me out of the hand of this Philistine" (1 Samuel 17:37).

5. *The Uncommon Warrior Knows That The Power Of God Is Greater Than The Weapons Of Man.* David did. "Then said David to the Philistine, Thou comest to me with a sword, and with a spear, and with a shield: but I come to thee in the name of the Lord of hosts, the God of the armies of Israel, Whom thou has defied" (1 Samuel 17:45).

6. *The Uncommon Warrior Often Uses, In His Greatest Battles, The Skills Developed In His Daily Routine.* David did. "And he took his staff in his hand, and chose him five smooth stones out of the brook, and put them in a shepherd's bag which he had, even in a scrip; and his sling was in his hand: and he drew near to the Philistine" (1 Samuel 17:40).

7. *The Uncommon Warrior Expects To Be An Instrument In The Hand Of God To Destroy His Enemy.* David did. He said, "and I will smite thee, and take thine head from thee; and I will give the carcases of the host of the Philistines this day unto the fowls of the air, and to the wild beasts of the earth; that all the earth may know that there is a God in Israel" (1 Samuel 17:46).

8. *The Uncommon Warrior Expects His Enemies To Fall And He Publicly Predicts His Victory.* David did. "This day will the Lord deliver thee into mine hand;" (1 Samuel 17:46). "When mine enemies are turned back, they shall fall and perish at Thy presence. For Thou hast maintained my right and my cause; Thou satest in the throne judging right. Thou hast rebuked the heathen, Thou has destroyed the wicked, Thou hast put out their name for ever and ever...But the Lord shall endure for ever:" (Psalm 9:3-5,7).

9. *The Uncommon Warrior Stays On The Offensive Running Toward His Enemy.* David did. "And it came to pass, when the Philistine arose, and came and drew nigh to meet David, that David hasted, and ran toward the army to meet the Philistine" (1 Samuel 17:48).

10. *The Uncommon Warrior Expects The Spectators Of The Battle To Observe And Experience The Power Of God.* David did. "And all this assembly shall know that the Lord saveth not with sword and spear: for the battle is the Lord's, and He will give you into our hands" (1 Samuel 17:47).

11. *The Uncommon Warrior Keeps Vibrant Memories Of Past Victories.* David did. "And David said unto Saul, The servant kept

his father's sheep, and there came a lion, and a bear, and took a lamb out of the flock: And I went out after him, and smote him, and delivered it out of his mouth: and when he arose against me, I caught him by his beard, and smote him, and slew him. Thy servant slew both the lion and the bear: and this uncircumcised Philistine shall be as one of them, seeing he hath defied the armies of the living God" (1 Samuel 17:34-36).

12. *The Uncommon Warrior Ignores The Opinions Of Obvious Losers And Failures Around Him.* David did. "And Eliab his eldest brother heard when he spake unto the men; and Eliab's anger was kindled against David, and he said, Why camest thou down hither? and with whom hast thou left those few sheep in the wilderness? I know thy pride, and the naughtiness of thine heart; for thou art come down that thou mightest see the battle. And David said, What have I now done? Is there not a cause? And he turned from him toward another, and spake after the same manner: and the people answered him again after the former manner" (1 Samuel 17:28-30).

13. *The Uncommon Warrior Pursues, Savors And Celebrates The Rewards Of Every Victory.* David did. "And David spake to the men that stood by him, saying, What shall be done to the man that killeth this Philistine, and taketh away the reproach from Israel? for who is this uncircumcised Philistine, that he should defy the armies of the living God?...it shall be, that the man who killeth him, the king will enrich him with great riches, and will give him his daughter, and make his father's house free in Israel" (1 Samuel 17:26,25).

14. *The Uncommon Warrior Keeps His Promise To Destroy His Enemy.* David did. "Therefore David ran, and stood upon the Philistine, and took his sword, and drew it out of the sheath thereof, and slew him, and cut off his head therewith" (1 Samuel 17:51).

15. *The Uncommon Warrior Unashamedly Displays The Spoils Of Past Victories As Trophies Of Thanksgiving.* David even carried the head of Goliath around with him. "And as David returned from the slaughter of the Philistine, Abner took him, and brought him before Saul with the head of the Philistine in his hand" (1 Samuel 17:57).

16. *The Uncommon Warrior Creates His Own Museum Of Memories To Celebrate His Victories.* David did. "And David took the head of the Philistine, and brought it to Jerusalem; but he put his armour in his tent" (1 Samuel 17:54).

17. *The Uncommon Warrior Knows That The Defeat Of His Strongest Adversary Will Cause His Other Enemies To Flee.* David saw this. When Goliath fell, his followers fled. "And when the Philistines saw their champion was dead, they fled" (1 Samuel 17:51).

18. *The Uncommon Warrior Knows That When He Is Victorious, The Discouraged Around Him Become Encouraged And Energized.* David saw this happen. "And the men of Israel and of Judah arose, and shouted, and pursued the Philistines, until thou come to the valley, and to the gates of Ekron. And the wounded of the Philistines fell down by the way to Shaaraim, even unto Gath, and unto Ekron" (1 Samuel 17:52).

Somebody else needs to see you win.

Preparation is the key to successful warfare.

Remember: *Your Assignment Will Require The Nature, Skills And Mentality Of A Warrior.*

Pray this special prayer aloud with me now:
"Holy Spirit, I am Your child.

Thank You for revealing Your Assignment to me today.

Empower me to seize it and pursue it boldly with my whole heart and life.

Connect me with a network of mentors and intercessors who can help me give birth to my next season.

I joyfully submit to Your authority, Your counsel and Your guidance and obey You with all my heart, mind and soul. In Jesus' name. Amen."

My Dear Reader...I would love to hear from you today!

Sit down now. Write me a brief note on how this revelation on *The Assignment* is changing your life. Feel free to share any special prayer requests that you have for the staff and me to pray over.

You matter to me greatly.

Thank you for sowing Seeds of your love, prayers and finances to help spread the Wisdom of God. Expect your Uncommon Seed to produce an Uncommon Harvest for you and your family.

Simply write: Mike Murdock · The Wisdom Center ·P.O. Box 99 · Denton, Texas 76202.

DR. MIKE MURDOCK

1 Has embraced his Assignment to Pursue...Proclaim...and Publish the Wisdom of God to help people achieve their dreams and goals.

2 Began full-time evangelism at the age of 19, which has continued since 1966.

3 Has traveled and spoken to more than 14,000 audiences in 38 countries, including East and West Africa, the Orient and Europe.

4 Noted author of over 130 books, including best sellers, *"Wisdom For Winning," "Dream Seeds"* and *"The Double Diamond Principle."*

5 Created the popular "Topical Bible" series for Businessmen, Mothers, Fathers, Teenagers; "The One-Minute Pocket Bible" series, and "The Uncommon Life" series.

6 Has composed more than 5,700 songs such as *"I Am Blessed," "You Can Make It," "God Rides On Wings Of Love"* and *"Jesus Just The Mention Of Your Name,"* recorded by many gospel artists.

7 Is the Founder of The Wisdom Center, in Denton, Texas.

8 Has a weekly television program called *"Wisdom Keys With Mike Murdock."*

9 Has appeared often on TBN, CBN, BET and other television network programs.

10 Is a Founding Trustee on the Board of International Charismatic Bible Ministries with Oral Roberts.

11 Has had more than 3,500 accept the call into full-time ministry under his ministry.

THE MINISTRY

1 **Wisdom Books & Literature** - Over 130 best-selling Wisdom Books and 70 Teaching Tape Series.

2 **Church Crusades** - Multitudes are ministered to in crusades and seminars throughout America in "The Uncommon Wisdom Conferences." Known as a man who loves pastors he has focused on church crusades for 36 years.

3 **Music Ministry** - Millions have been blessed by the anointed songwriting and singing of Mike Murdock, who has made over 15 music albums and CDs available.

4 **Television** - "Wisdom Keys With Mike Murdock," a nationally-syndicated weekly television program.

5 **The Wisdom Center** - The Ministry Offices of The Mike Murdock Evangelistic Association where Schools of Wisdom have been held.

6 **Schools of the Holy Spirit** - Mike Murdock hosts Schools of the Holy Spirit in many churches to mentor believers on the Person and Companionship of the Holy Spirit.

7 **Schools of Wisdom** - In many major cities Mike Murdock hosts Schools of Wisdom for those who want personalized and advanced training for achieving "The Uncommon Dream."

8 **Missions Outreach** - Dr. Murdock's overseas outreaches to 38 countries have included crusades in East and West Africa, South America, the Orient and Europe.

Personal Notes

Personal Notes